TWO ALPHA LIMA

TWO ALPHA LIMA

The First Ten Years of the Trucial Oman Levies and Trucial Oman Scouts (1950 to 1960)

PETER CLAYTON

JANUS PUBLISHING COMPANY
London, England

First published in Great Britain 1994
by Janus Publishing Company
Edinburgh House, 19 Nassau Street
London W1N 7RE

British Library Cataloguing-in-Publication Data
A catalogue record for this book is available
from the British Library

ISBN 1 85756 196 1

Printed and bound in Great Britain by
Antony Rowe Ltd, Chippenham, Wiltshire

Contents

Illustrations

Acknowledgements

In addition to those who encouraged me to make this record and have put up with my obsession with the work over some years, my thanks go to the many who have submitted to my interrogation and for their hospitality whilst undergoing it, in the United Kingdom and the United Arab Emirates.

They include: General Abdulla Ali al Ka'abi, General Ahmed Salim al Ka'abi, Colonel John Ansell, Mr Ali Azayz bin Maktoom, Mr Ali Bati Eisa, Mr Noel Ayliffe-Jones, the late Lieut-Col Colin Barnes, Dr Charles Binns, the late Major Tim Budd, Colonel Stewart Carter, Major Desmond Cosgrove, the late Major Ian Craig-Adams, Shaikh Faisal Sultan al Qasimi, Lieut-Col Tony Gibb, Mr Hassan Abdullah Noman, Mr Edward Henderson, Mr Ismail Saddiq Othman, Colonel Eric Johnson, General Khilfan Matr al Rumaithi, Colonel Bob Martin, Mr Mohammed Nakhaira bin Mahroom, Colonel Mohammed Saleh, General Obaid Ali Rashid, Captain Simon Portal, Major John Pott, General Said Abdulla Ali, Major Tony Steggles and Major Jim Stockdale.

My thanks, too, to Mrs Birchall for permission to use photographs from the late Captain Theo Birchall's collection for plates 33, 34, 35 and 36. The remaining photographs and sketch maps are mine as are all the mistakes and errors.

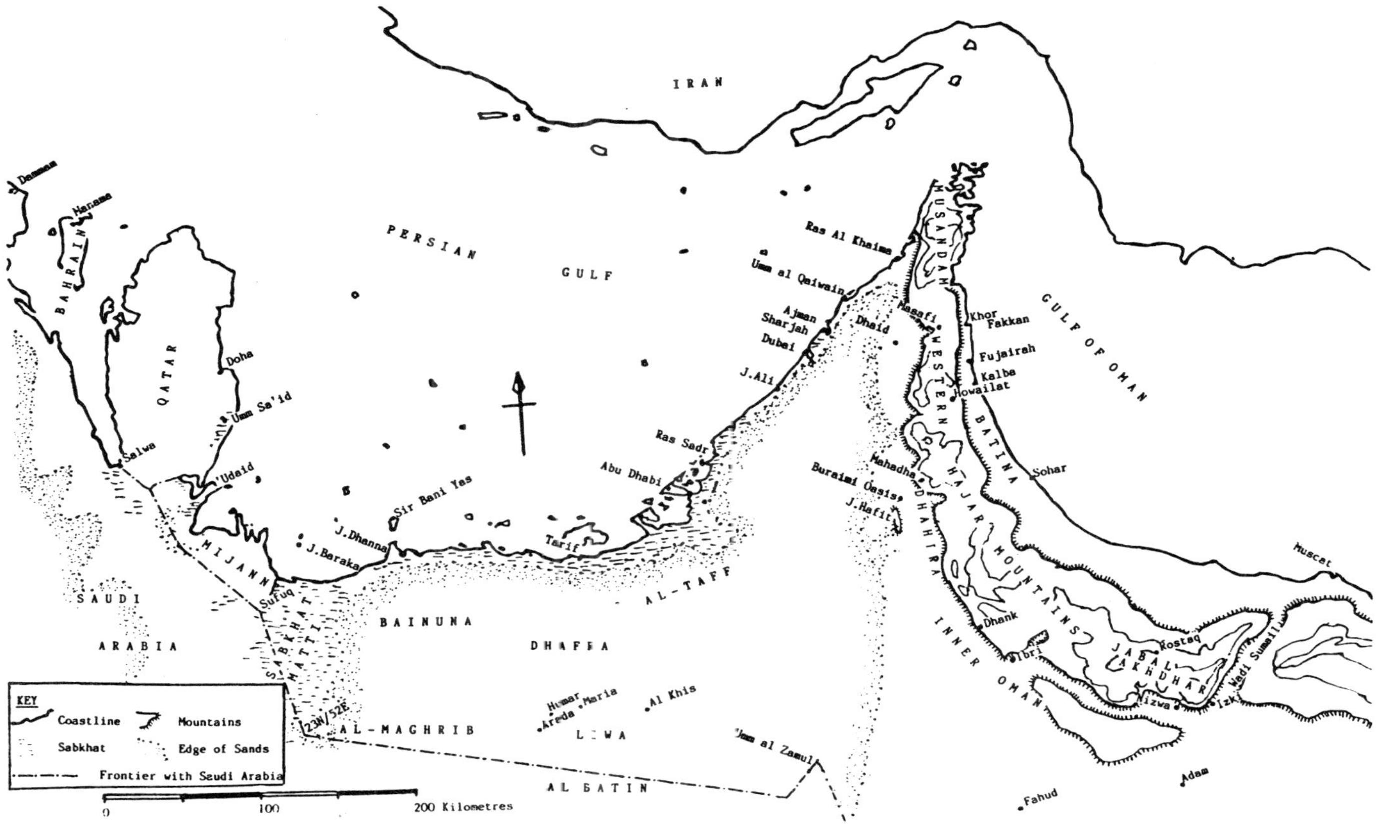

Trucial States and Oman – whole area of operations

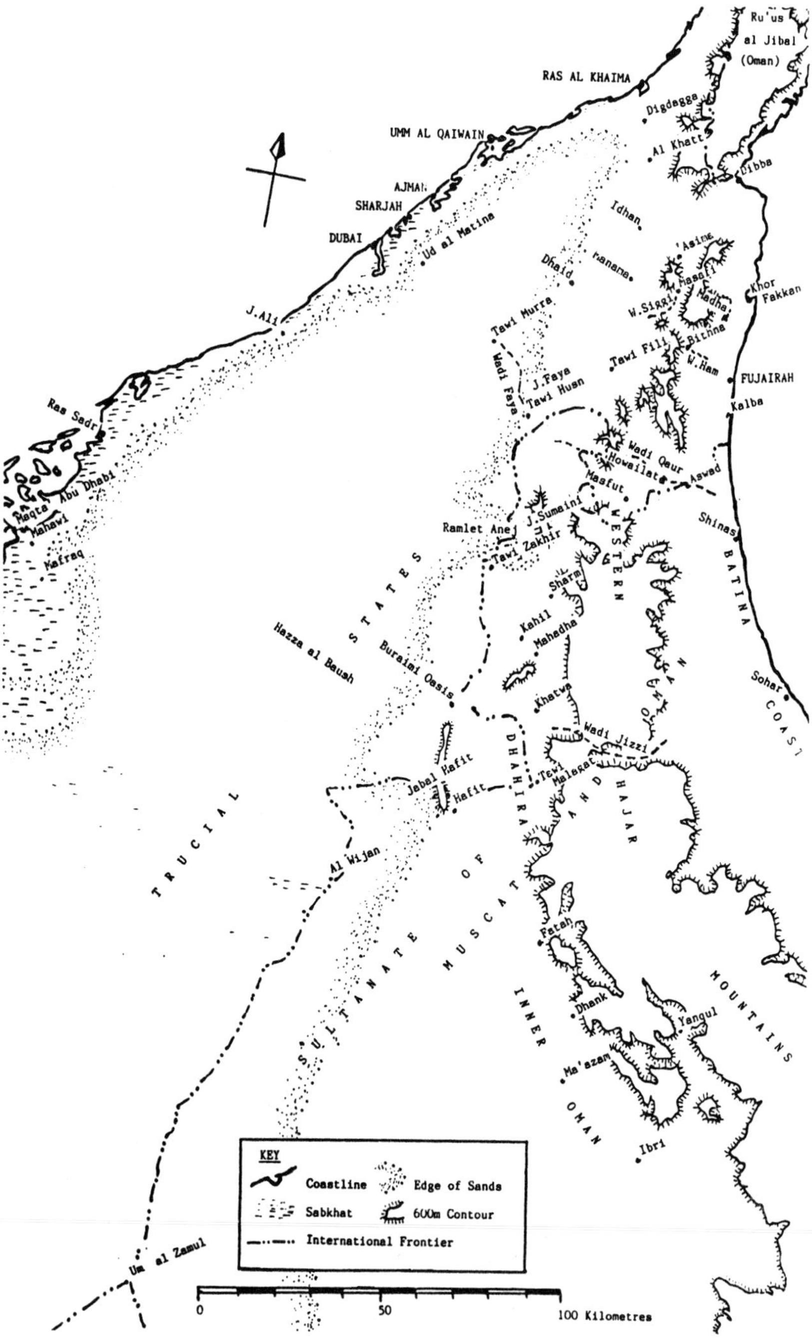

Eastern area – Batina to Abu Dhabi, including Ibri

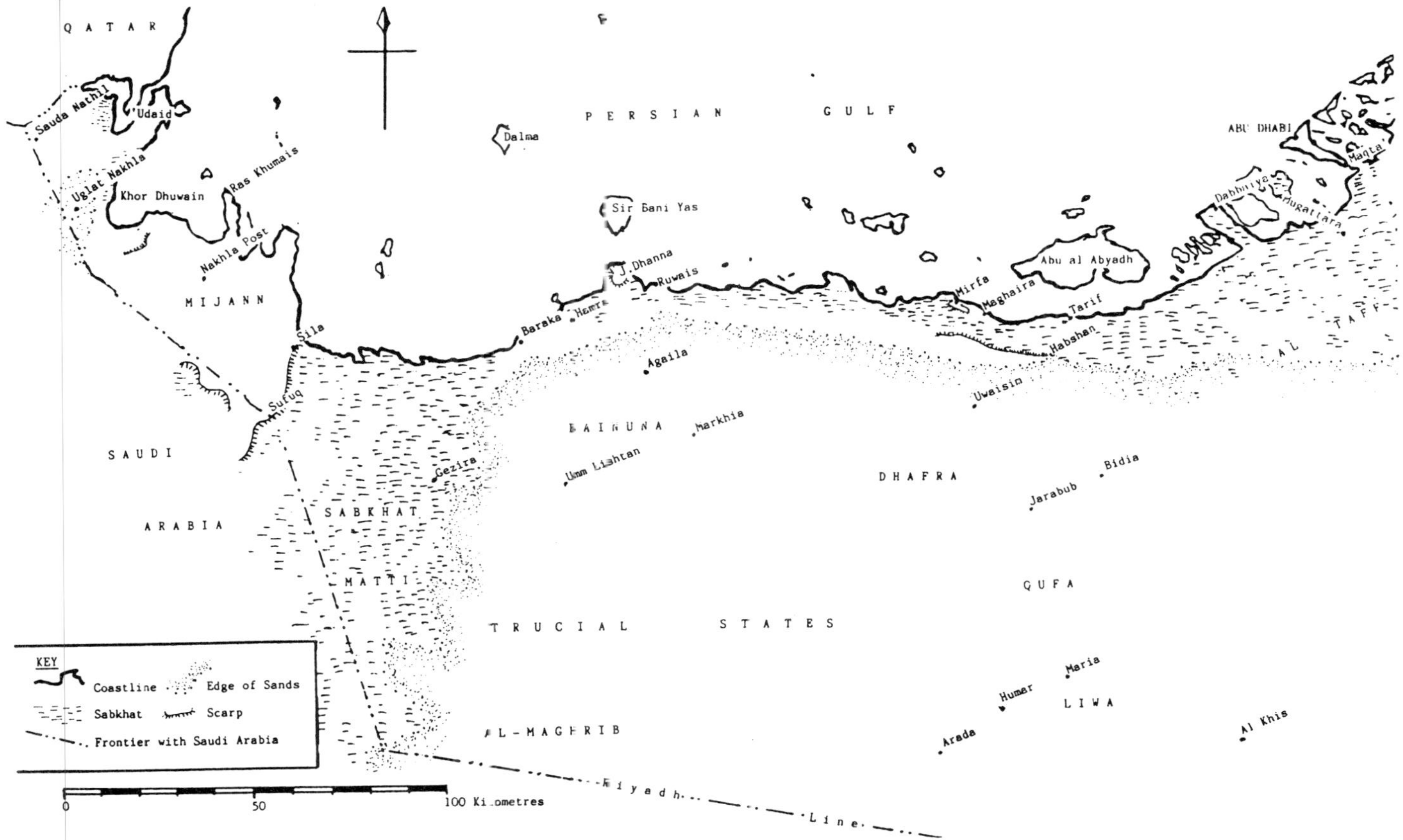

Western area – Abu Dhabi to Qatar, including Liwa

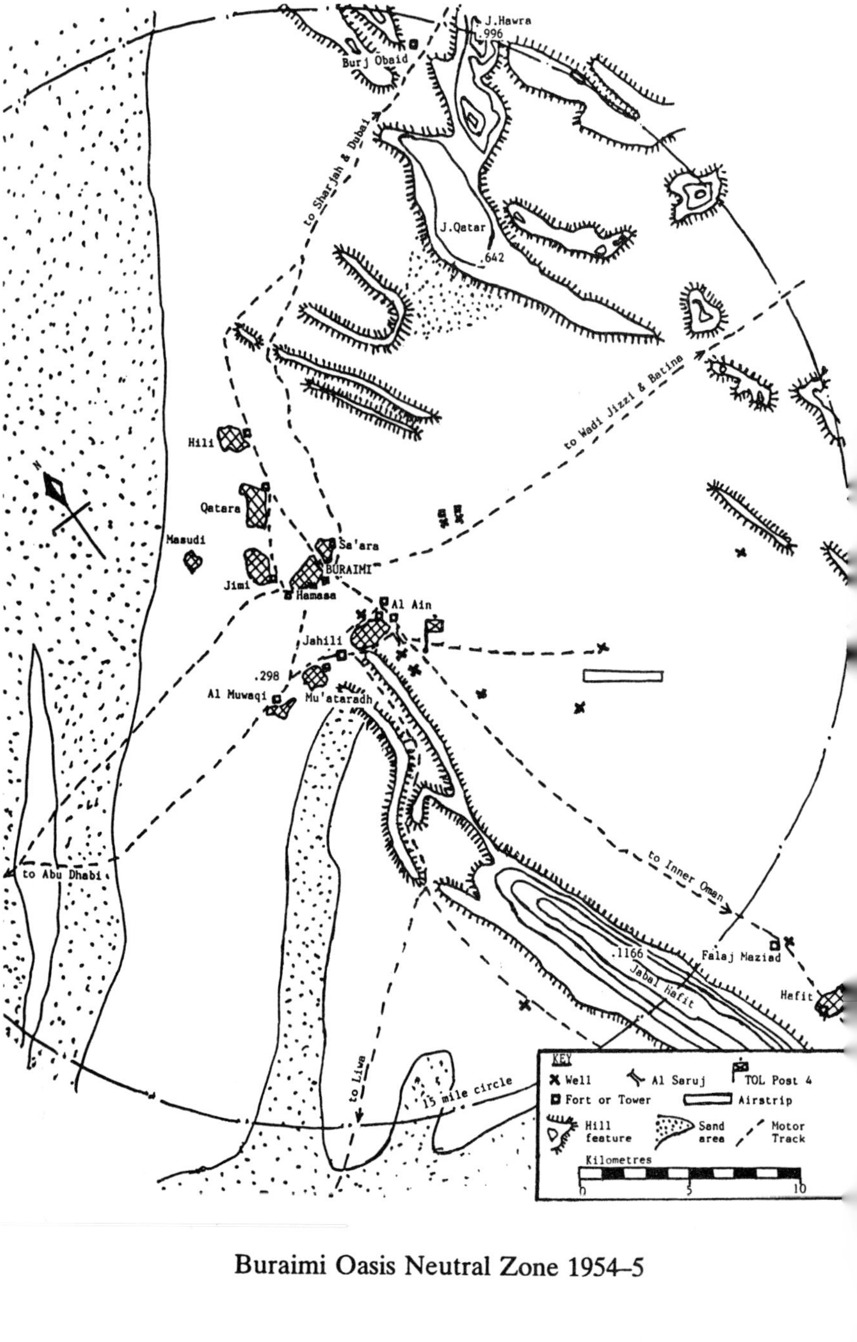

Buraimi Oasis Neutral Zone 1954–5

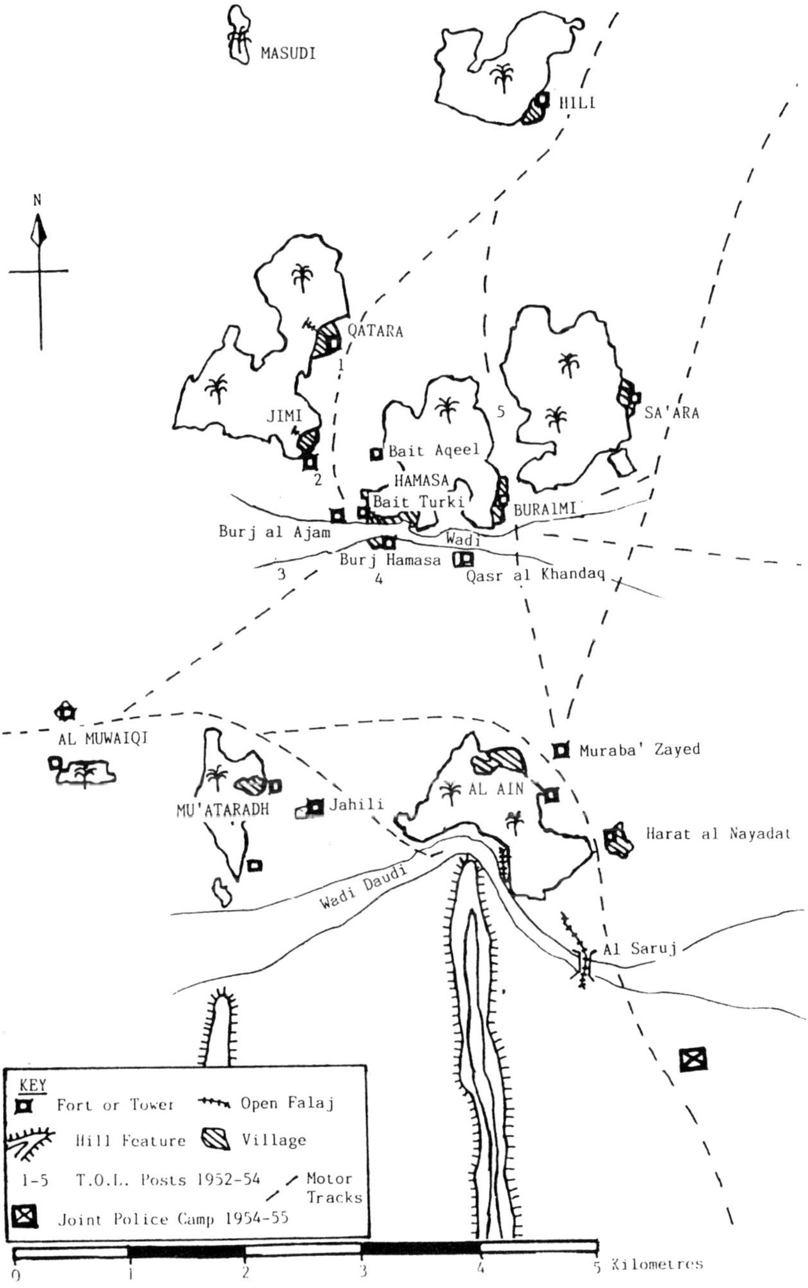

Buraimi Oasis operational locations 1953–4 and 1955

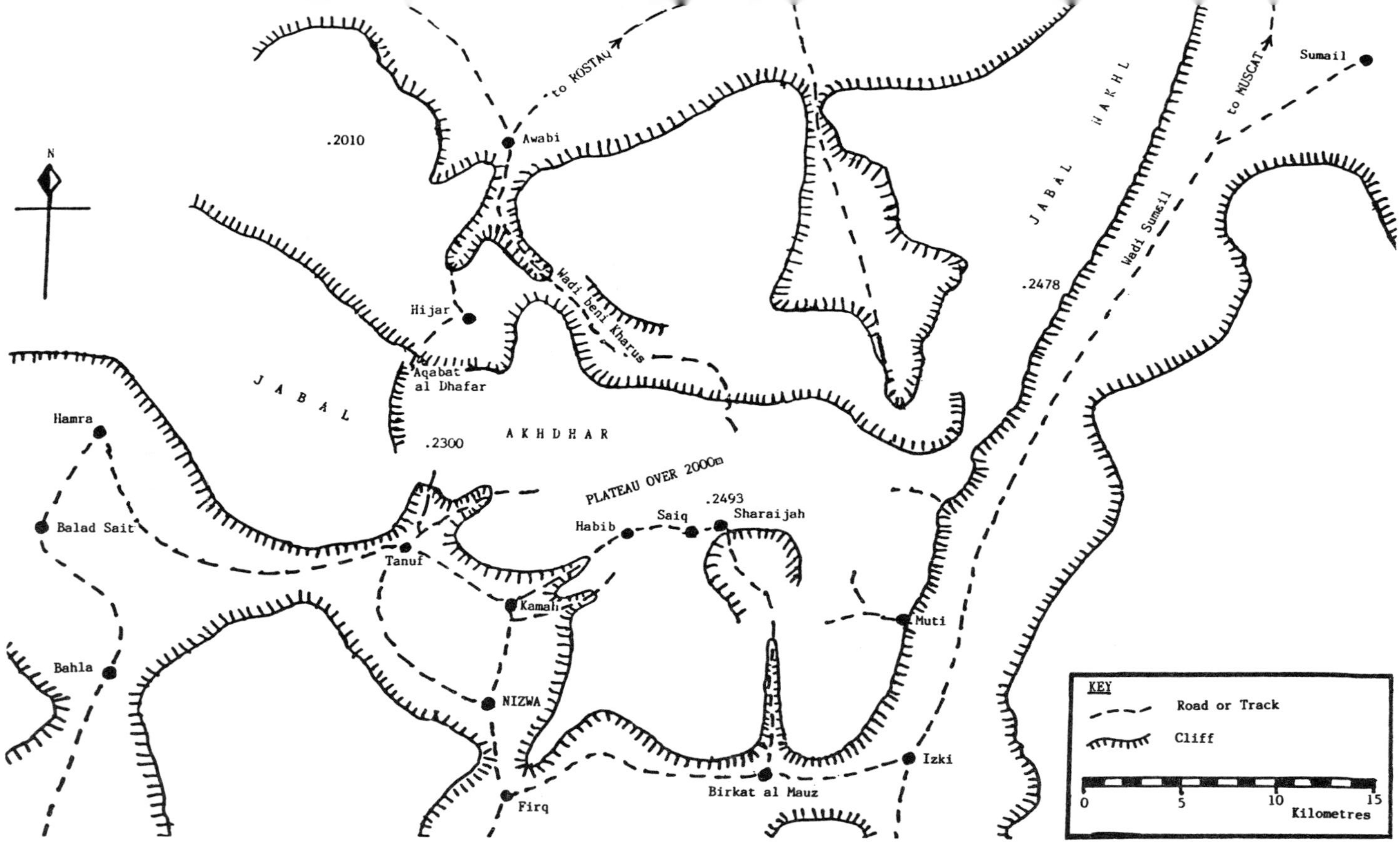

Jabal Akhdhar operational area 1957 and 1958–9

Introduction

This record of the first ten years of the history of the unit is presented as a progressively unfolding Intelligence report, with personal annecdotes and comments, in strict chronological order of events.

Great Britain has been in treaty relations with the Rulers of the tribal areas on the shores of the South Eastern Arabian Peninsula and the Persian Gulf since 1798 in the case of the Sultan of Muscat and Oman, and since 1820 with the Gulf-coastal Rulers including Bahrain. These treaties came about from the need to secure the sea routes to India from piracy. In return for abstaining from raids upon British and East India Company shipping, the litoral tribes were to come under British protection in case of attack from external third parties. In broad terms, the General Treaty of Peace of 1820 ensured that the area would remain under British influence to the exclusion of the Portugese and French. The British had no jurisdiction within the territory apart from the establishment of a temporary garrison at Ras al Khaima in 1820 and the appointment by the Government of Bombay of a Native Agent to reside in Sharjah to represent British interests in about 1825. In May 1853, all the Rulers signed the Perpetual Treaty of Peace which gave rise to the name Trucial Coast to replace the previous references to the Pirate Coast.

The opening up of the air route from Britain to India and beyond in the 1930s resulted in the establishment by the Royal Air Force and Imperial Airways of the airfield at Sharjah and the construction of the fort there as the protected overnight resthouse and refuelling station. In 1937, the British Government defined, to their own satisfaction presumably, the border of the Trucial States with the Kingdom of Saudi Arabia.

Flying boats used this air route during the Second World War so the facilities were extended by the development of the upper part of Dubai creek for their landings and take-offs and the construction of a jetty on its northern shore. To protect the bases at Sharjah and Muscat, local men were enlisted, trained, armed and put into uniform. They were collectively referred to as the Muscat Levies and were disbanded at the end of the war. The British service personnel stationed on the Trucial Coast were confined to their base and were not in contact with local inhabitants apart from those employed on the base itself.

After the Second World War ended, the serious exploration for oil started in South East Arabia. Over the next five years the territory was surveyed by geologists in motor vehicles. The negotiations between the oil companies and the tribal leaders about concessions to explore and drill for oil gave rise to territorial claims and counter-claims between the Rulers themselves and involved the neighbouring states of Qatar, the Sultanate of Muscat and Oman and the Kingdom of Saudi Arabia. These disputes came to a head in 1949 and the need arose for an increased British involvement on the ground to meet their treaty obligations to the Trucial States Rulers. In particular was the need for the, by then, British Foreign Office officials to visit remote tribal chiefs inland and to assist them in the maintenance of law and order if required. In addition, the 'Truce' was intended to discourage the slave trade. To protect the British officials in their task, it was decided at that time that a small force of Arab troops would be adequate and also mitigate against the accusation of British imperialism then fashionable in the Arab world and elsewhere. The most suitable source of men for such a force was the British-trained Jordanian Arab Legion whose recent achievements in the Palestine war were in their favour. In addition, there were ancient tribal links with Jordan that did not exist with the Kurds and Assyrians of the RAF Iraqi Levies or with the Adenese of the RAF Aden Protectorate Levies.

A small number of seconded Jordanian Arab Legionaries, who were sent as the nucleus of this force of 'armed police', arrived at the beginning of 1951 under the control of the British Foreign Office. They were not able to oppose the incursion from Saudi Arabia into the Buraimi Oasis in 1952. Locally recruited troops were reinforced by mercenaries from Aden with tragic results. The Buraimi Dispute ended in 1955 with the re-occupation of Hamasa by the Trucial Oman Levies. A period of growth and reorganisation followed until the outbreak of the revolt in Oman in the summer of 1957. By then called the Trucial Oman Scouts, they were sent to assist the Sultan's

Armed Forces and recaptured Nizwa with them and British troops. The lessons learnt in this campaign brought about further changes in time for the Second Oman Campaign in 1958–9 when they took part in the operations to capture the Jabal Akhdhar. The last years of the decade were spent in consolidating further growth against a background of increasing destabilisation in South East Arabia.

The source of documented information was the Public Records Office at Kew in Surrey, for those records released after the thirty-year period. These were found to contain only those papers dealing with topics of a 'non-sensitive' nature. The reports of most Local Defence Committee meetings have been held back for fifty or more years.[1] Likewise, no Local Intelligence Committee meeting records are available.[2] Nevertheless this research has provided the basic historical framework and some full reports of the unit's activities. The filling in of details of events has been by interviews with participants, both Arab and British and by reference to published works.

I served with the unit for over two years from January 1954 as a squadron commander, on special duties, and as patrol-force commander in various outstations. I was then appointed the first Political and Intelligence Officer of the Trucial Oman Scouts from March 1956 to March 1957. During this time, I also raised and commanded the Dubai Police Force.

In August 1959, I returned to the area on the staff of the Headquarters Land Forces Persian Gulf in Bahrain as Senior Desert Intelligence Officer.

Notes

1 The Local Defence Committee (LDC) was chaired by the British Political Resident with the senior British officers of all three armed services in his area of control and any forces temporarily present. Political and Intelligence staff attended. The LDC met usually in the Residency in Bahrain on a regular schedule.

2 The Local Intelligence Committee (LIC) was chaired by a member of the Political Resident's staff and attended by all available Intelligence Officers. Routine meetings were held at regular intervals wherever most members could assemble. Special meetings took place where and when required.

1

Topography, Population and Speech of the Trucial States

Topography

The region now comprises the seven Emirates of the United Arab Emirates (UAE) together with the enclaves of the Sultanate of Oman in the mountain region, as far south as Buraimi. This whole area was called the Trucial Oman. The Trucial Coast was the name of the Persian Gulf coast, and the Batina Coast is that part of the Trucial Oman facing the Gulf of Oman (see Map 1).

The terrain is of two main types: the desert region in the west and the eastern mountains with their sub-montane outwash plains. The western desert (see Map 3) corresponds roughly to the Emirate of Abu Dhabi and consists of the northern coastal plain of *sabkhat* (salt flats) broken here and there by low rocky *mezas*. Off the shore, there is a line of low-lying islands among coral reefs and sand bars. Inland, the ground rises in a series of low ridges of the same soft rock with gravel and *sabkhat* inlets. Further inland the sand cover increases in the Dhafra region until the great yellow and orange dunes of the Liwa rise to over 150 metres. In the Liwa a long necklace of hollows running east-west makes up the oasis. Here there are sweet-water wells supporting a few small palm groves under constant threat from the dunes. The prevailing wind is from the north moving the dunes slowly southwards over the whole area.

Southwards from Jabal Dhanna stretches the Bainuna, an area of low, rolling gravel hills and shallow, sand-filled valleys. There are a few widely dispersed wells of slightly brackish water, as at Agaila and Umm Lishtan, and a scattering of camel scrub bushes. To the south of the Bainuna lies the Al-Mughrib area of low to medium height dunes, mainly light in colour aligned east-west but with no wells of any permanence.

At the western end of the Trucial Coast (see Map 3), the Sabkhat Matti reaches southwards from the sea for over 100 kilometres. This area of *sabkhat* is interspersed with low sand fields and is devoid of any wells. Further west again, the Mijann plateau rises with a low but steep scarp from the flats of the Sabkhat Matti. This mainly gravel plateau is broken up by shallow *wadis* running north to the rocky shore with many inlets. The few wells in the area are brackish. Apart from a group of trees to the north of Sila this gravel area is without vegetation other than occasional camel scrub bushes in the sandy *wadi* beds. The strip of territory running up to the border with Qatar is a mixture of *sabkhat* and dune belts of the 'Uqal leading up to the low rocky *mezas* and limestone hills of the 'Udaid peninsula.

The eastern region (see Map 2) is dominated by the (Western) Hajar Mountains of varied geological make up. Dark jagged basalt and wind-eroded fawn limestone ridges are cut by *wadis*, their dry water courses filled with brown boulders and clay mud pans. When rain falls these *wadis* flood quickly. There are a number of villages in the main *wadis* and in the foothills. The general 'grain' of the mountains is north-south with gaps in the ridges giving only a few east-west through routes. The deep *wadi* beds themselves provided the communication routes as the sedimentary gravel flats are cut by steep-sided tributary water courses.

There were two motor tracks through the Hajar Mountains to the Batina Coast at this period: the Wadi Qaur passing Howailat to Aswad on the border with the Sultanate and the Wadi Jizzi from the Buraimi Oasis through to Sohar.

The watershed between the Wadi Siggi east of Masafi and the Wadi Ham above Al Bithna was passable by camels as was a route to Dibba. The Wadi Hatta motor route reached Masfut but did not lead through to the Batina.

The outwash plains to the west of the mountains are of clay and gravel. Sweet-water wells are widely separated on this plain that runs from Ras al Khaima in the north to the Ramlet Anej. The *ghaf* trees gave the area a sparsely wooded savanna-like appearance. These trees provided firewood for the population of a wide area and the plain itself was grazed by the goats and camels of the *bedu*. Herds of gazelle were to be found there too.

The sand cover increases westwards away from the mountains but corridors of gravel plain (*sih*) and the Wadi Faya that drains westwards into the sands, provide routes from the coast to the mountains. The sands meet the mountains south of Jabal Sumaini and form the Ramlet Anej barrier.

South of this barrier, the Wadi Sharm and the foothills to the north of Jabal Qatar enclose an area of gravel plain and low rocky ridges before the plain opens out again to the east of the Buraimi Oasis. This sub-montane plain, the Dhahira, has to the west the isolated 1,200-metre-high whaleback of Jabal Hafit. Further south the Western Hajar Mountains swing to the south-east and Inner Oman whilst the edge of the sands continue southwards. Long, flat gravel fingers penetrate west-north-west into the sands reaching the undefined border between the Sultanate and the Trucial States.

Camel caravan trails led from well to well, though certain areas of *sabkhat* such as the Sabkhat Matti and the coastal *sabkhat* flats were avoided. Well packed *sabkhat* can carry wheeled traffic in dry weather but weakens when the water table below it rises. The rolled *sabkhat* runway at RAF Sharjah airbase would become unusable after a combination of winter rains and a high tide with a north wind in the Gulf.

A motorable route ran, in the early 1950s, along the coast linking Ras al Khaima, to Sharjah and Dubai, Jabal Ali, Mafraq Abu Dhabi, Tarif, Ruwais, Baraka, the Sabkhat Matti and on to the Mijann at Sila, and into Saudi Arabia. It ran inland of the *sabkhat* where possible. Where used by the oil company it was sometimes 'graded' when the corrugations (*jumbeeng*) became too severe. Elsewhere the track was left to spread and wander where it became rough or too soft.

The motor routes to the inland oases of Dhaid and Buraimi from Sharjah and Dubai crossed the sands between the lines of dune crests either almost directly east to Dhaid or somewhat more southerly passing the well at Ud Al Matina to Jabal Al Faya. Here the track forked east through the Wadi Qaur to the Batina and Muscat or south along the gravel plain and over the Ramlet Anej to Buraimi and Inner Oman. The motor route between Abu Dhabi and the Buraimi Oasis followed the grain of the land between the dunes until it crossed the sand barrier at Hazza Al Baush.

After rain or sand storms, many motor routes needed to be cleared of boulders in the mountain *wadis* or rediscovered over the sands. The motor routes in the sands often followed camel caravan routes. When the vehicle tracks had been obliterated by blown sand, the faint shape of the camel droppings along the way could be seen by an experienced driver and followed. Camel carvans of one hundred camels, coming from Inner Oman to Buraimi and on to Sharjah and

Dubai, with charcoal and dates and returning with loads of 'shop goods', were common and provided a sufficient supply of camel droppings on the way.

For most of the period between 1950 and 1960 also, because of the unpredictable state of the *sabkhat* on the approach to the ford (later a causeway), onto the island of Abu Dhabi, passenger and goods traffic went by sea from Dubai or Sharjah rather than overland. The sea route between Sharjah or Ras al Khaima to Khor Fakkan and beyond on the Batina Coast, was often used in preference to the Wadi Qaur route, where there was the risk of banditry and the need to pass through the Sultanate customs post at Aswad.

Up until the end of 1960, there was not one metre of tarmac or concrete roadway anywhere in the territory.

Population of the Trucial Oman

The recruits for the Trucial Oman Levies and Scouts came mostly from the nomadic camel-dependant tribes of the desert; the date and goat-dependant shepherding tribes of the oases and the sub-montane plains; and from the hill tribes of the Western Hajar Mountains. The historical rivalries and alliances between the clans and tribes were usually ignored once the tribesmen had enlisted.

The general distribution and pattern of movement of the main tribal groups and sections follow in broad outline only.

In the west, the nomadic Manasir moved around in the Sabkhat Matti, Al Maghrib, Mijann and Bainuna areas. Another section of the Manasir were to be found inland, south of Jabal Ali.

The Bani Yas group of tribes inhabit the Liwa and used to migrate to the Dhafrah, join the pearling fleet and cross to the east to the Buraimi Oasis. The ruling families of Abu Dhabi and of Dubai are of the Al Bu Falah and Al Bu Falasa sections of the Bani Yas respectively. The many sub-tribes of the Bani Yas are to be found throughout the Trucial Coast and on the islands.

The Manahil are to be found along the southern border of the Liwa and Al Batin stretching eastwards towards Um al Zamul.

The Awamir spread from the eastern part of the Liwa across into the plains to the east of the border with the Sultanate of Oman. They are related to the tribes of the same name in the north and south of the Arabian Peninsula.

The Na'im are part settled and part nomadic throughout the sub-montane region between Ajman, where the rulers are of the Al Bu

Kharaiban section, and Hafit where the Khawtir live. The inhabitants of Buraimi and Sa'ara villages are almost exclusively from the Na'im.

The Al Bu Shamis separated from the Na'im and their *bedu* section live in the Qabil and Sanaina area. One of their main settlements is Hamasa in the Buraimi Oasis.

The Bani Qitab live in the Dhairah plains of Inner Oman well to the south of Jabal Hafit. They are also found on the northern plain between Dhaid and Tawi Fili.

The Bani Ka'ab live around Mahadha in the foothills of the Hajar in the Sultanate of Oman.

The Bani Ka'ab, the Bani Qitab and the Na'im have rarely been on good terms with each other, leading to an undercurrent of unrest in the hinterland between the sands and the mountains.

The Dhawahir are mainly pastoral living in and around the Abu Dhabi villages of the Buraimi Oasis.

In the coastal towns lived people of mixed origin, from all around the southern Persian Gulf coast and both sides of the Gulf of Oman. They were known, certainly by the *bedu* tribesmen, as 'Balushis' as distinct from the Baluch of Baluchistan or Makran.

The tribe of the Baluch in the Ma'azam area in Inner Oman did originate from Baluchistan many generations ago.

Those of direct Persian descent living in the towns, generally as merchants and pearl traders were known as Ajamis.

After interviewing a few hundred potential recruits for the Trucial Oman Scouts (TOS) and for the Dubai Police and asking them for details of their tribe, clan and where they had come from, I, as the TOS Intelligence Officer became aware of the distinct characteristics of facial appearance, manner of speaking and general bearing of the major tribal groups.

The total population was estimated in the late 1950s as between 50,000 and 80,000 of whom less than 25,000 inhabited Dubai and Deira and perhaps 10,000 were nomadic *bedu*. The remainder lived in the oases, coastal towns and villages, the mountain villages and were pastoral or fishermen. With a population this size, the mobile nomadic people, who identified and spoke to all they met, appeared to know everyone. The settled folk knew their neighbours and gossiped about everybody they knew. With no radio and no television the only entertainment was conversation.

The foreign, now 'ex-patriate', population was small. There was a long-established Indian merchant community. The members of these trading families moved around the branches of the businesses, spending a few years in perhaps Dubai, Kuwait, Bahrain and returning mostly to Bombay. The British RAF personnel in the base at Sharjah varied in numbers but were completely isolated, remaining within the confines of the camp. The European oil-company staff were also self-contained in their desert camps, either at the rig sites or in the field exploration parties.

The resident European population in Abu Dhabi in early 1957 was three, the Political Agent, Mr Martin Buckmaster, and Mr Tim Hillyard and his wife, of the Abu Dhabi Marine Areas oil company (ADMA).

In Sharjah, the Desert Locust Survey had a house at the eastern end of the town where their representative sometimes stayed.[1] There were seasonal visits from a pair of American missionary doctors who had a central clinic-cum-residence. In the BOAC Fort were the International Aeradio Limited manager, Mr Sydney Hodge, and sometimes one or two members of his staff.[2] From 1953, Colonel Martin, Commandant of the Trucial Oman Levies, lived with his wife and two children in a house on the creekside at the western end of the *suq*.

From 1953 Dubai was the location of the British Political Agency with the Political Agent and one or two Political Officers. The Manager of the British Bank of the Middle East with his family and a few members of staff, Mr George Chapman of Grey Mackenzie the shipping agents, Dr Desmond McCaulley OBE of the Maktoum Hospital in Deira, the Petroleum Development Trucial Coast (PDTC) representatives, including Mr Ron Codrai and Mr Edward Henderson, made up the rest of the community.[3]

The Speech of the Trucial Oman

The most noticeable feature of the spoken Arabic of the Trucial States is that it is at the opposite end of the phonetic 'spectrum' from the hard Ds, Gs and Qs of further west, but retains a full value for each letter sound and does not drop the letter Qaf to an 'Ain as in the Levant; so coffee is *Qahwa* not the lazy *Ahwa*. The 'Ain is pronounced correctly.

However, some of the hard consonants are noticeably softened, for example, the Qaf in the place name now spelt Shariqa, is pronounced 'Sharja'. The Qaf becoming a J. This is also found when the Qaf is at the end of the word, *tariq* (way or route) becomes *toreej*, *rafiq* (companion) becomes *rafeej*. For a long time, the Qawasim were known to the world as the 'Jawasim' or 'Jassimees'.

The letter Jeem is often lightened to a strong Y (as in French *papillion*). On Saudi Arabian maps, the Liwa is spelt Al Juwa. Al Mijann is pronounced 'Al Miyyan', the people of the Najadat tribe are 'Neyyadis' and, of course, a *falaj* is a '*falayy*'.

The letter Kaf becomes 'Ch' so *Kayf khalak?* (How are you?) becomes *Chief khalak?* when the Beni Yas greet each other.

The vocabulary used throughout the Trucial States before the advent of the transistor radio in the mid–1950s contained a number of words in common usage that were not in the standard Arabic dictionaries published in Beirut, or if included, had the note 'archaic' against them. The specialised jargon of the camel-dependant *bedu* is perhaps still unrecorded.

Within the TOL and the TOS, there grew up a dialect made up of some Adeni words, expressions borrowed from Jordan, Sudanese encouragements and standard British Army expletives. I was once called upon to resolve a misunderstanding between an exasperated British NCO instructor and an indignant Arab other-rank student who objected to the former using the fifth form (reflexive) of the root word *fkn*. At one time, each squadron, after a month or so in outstations developed their own argot, reflecting the style and origin of the Arabic spoken by their squadron commander. Major Budd's A Squadron used Nilotic phrases from the Sudan Defence Force, in Major Craig-Adam's C Squadron, Malay words, from his time with the Malayan Regiment, were understood and the soldiers in those sub-units with newly joined British officers had to use all the English they knew in order to communicate.

Notes

1 The Desert Locust Survey organisation had been operating under British Government sponsorship in Arabia since 1943–4. Wilfred Thesiger was attached to them for his travels in the Empty Quater in 1948–9. In the early 1950s, locust swarms reached the Trucial States and destroyed crops in the Liwa in 1951. Throughout the 1950s, a Desert Locust Survey officer, Mr Len Tilling, was based in Sharjah at certain times of the year. In the spring of 1954, locusts were plentiful at Tarif and Maghaira.

2 International Aeradio Limited (IAL) provided the aviation radio network and air-traffic control throughout the Gulf. In Sharjah, they operated from the old BOAC Fort built for Imperial Airways in 1932. The Fort had about 15 bedrooms, a restaurant and a lounge for transit pas-

sengers. It provided overflow accommodation for the Trucial Oman Levies' visitors and the only alternative venue for officers' private parties.

3 Mr Edward Henderson arrived in Dubai in 1948 as the resident representative of PDTC in the Trucial States and Muscat and Oman. He had previously spent two years with the Arab Legion in Jordan. In 1953, he was transferred to Bahrain to gather information on the Buraimi Dispute. He also visited Muscat and Salala in preparation for the landing of the Muscat Field Force (MFF) at Duqm which he accompanied. In September 1954, he took an important part in the MFF advance to Fahud that resulted in their recapture of Ibri. Again in Bahrain until October 1955, he was sent by the Political Resident as his representative with the TOL on the Hamasa operation to evict the Saudi Arabian party and its supporters. He stayed in Al Ain until the summer of 1956 when his secondment to the Foreign Office was extended until 1959. He entered the Foreign Service as Political Officer in Abu Dhabi until 1960. He returned to the Gulf in 1966 and became Political Agent in Qatar and was made Ambassador there in 1971 until 1974. Since that time he has lived mainly in Abu Dhabi.

2

1950

January

On 24 January 1950, the Treasury wrote to the Foreign Office agreeing to the formation 'of a small body of armed police' in the Trucial Shaikhdoms:

> to protect Political Officers touring in areas outside the Rulers' control,
> to assist the Rulers to maintain Law and Order,
> to assist the Rulers to fulfill their obligations with regard to slave traffic.[1]

The expenditure of £35,500 was under the heading of 'Persian Gulf Levy Force – Financial Regulation by the Foreign Office'. The funding was to be totally by the Foreign Office, and all equipment was to be purchased from the War Office.[2]

The force was to be commanded by Major J M Hankin-Turvin on a three-year contract and to have a cadre of 35 officers and other ranks on detachment from the Arab Legion in Jordan and 30 local recruits.[3]

The equipment authorised to be provided was:

50 x Rifles .303 inch, No 4
4 x Light Machine Guns .303 inch, BREN
2 x Mortars 2 inch, OML
5 x Pistols .38 inch, Revolver
3 x Pistols 1 inch, Signal
2 x Rifles .22 inch
6 x Trucks ¼ ton 4 x , Landrover
4 x Trucks 3 ton 4 x , Bedford QL
2 x Wireless Set No 19, High Power
2 x Wireless Set No 19, Low Power

May

In May 1950 there was a meeting at RAF Habbaniya, Iraq, to authorise the repair of 'the Levies' Camp' by the RAF at Sharjah. This refers to the buildings used by the locally raised armed guards employed during the Second World War to protect the airfield.

The Levies' Camp was a group of single-storey barrack huts built of thick panels of compressed reeds known as 'Basra Board' for the walls and partitions, which were fixed to a framework of *chandal* poles set into concrete floors.[4] Wooden framed doors and windows were covered with fine mesh as flyscreens and the roof was of double-pitched, corrugated metal sheet with ridge ventilators. The long side walls were shaded by open verandahs. Electric lighting was fitted but air conditioning was unknown. The Levies' camp was sited within the perimeter of the RAF base, on the eastern side with an external gate opening out onto the tracks across the sand and gravel.[5]

September

In September 1950, the Foreign Office reported to the Treasury that there had been numerous delays but that the force was expected to begin to function shortly.

King Abdulaziz ibn Saud had already raised objections through diplomatic channels to the formation of this force.

Oil exploration by the PDTC had started again after the end of the Second World War and this led to the questioning of the border between the kingdom of Saudi Arabia and the states of Abu Dhabi and Qatar. In 1949, the Arabian American Oil Company (ARAMCO), from Dhahran in Saudi Arabia, surveyed the coastal strip of Abu Dhabi territory from 'Udaid to Abu Dhabi Island itself. This brought the matter to a head and, in July 1950, the British and Saudi governments agreed to establish a Joint Technical Commission to investigate the tribal loyalties and the sovereignties of the Rulers in the disputed areas. This Commission failed to materialise.

The frontier recognised by the British Government on behalf of the Ruler of Abu Dhabi was the Riyadh Line, as amended in 1937, running from Sauda Nathil to the west of Khor 'Udaid, around the Mijann to a point on its eastern edge above a well then known as Sufuq, southwards to latitude 23 North, longtitude 52 East, at the southernmost point of the Sabkhat Matti, thence south of the Liwa to Um al Zumul (see Map 1).

The frontier claimed by the Saudi Government started at the coast at Mirfa, ran inland to the south-east to a point north of Habshan, thence direct to the Buraimi Oasis which was the core of their claim. The zone between these two lines was referred to as the 'Disputed Territory' (see Map 3).

Within the Trucial Shaikhdoms themselves, the concessions for oil exploration that had been granted to PDTC by the various Rulers since 1935 had come to assume great importance in their relations with each other. There were many internal frontier disputes between them and even a war between Dubai and Abu Dhabi, which started in 1945 and was finally settled in 1949 with the involvement of the British Government. The delineation of any internal frontiers was a matter for the future that would have to wait until after it was safe for the 'Political Officers to tour the areas outside the Ruler's control'.

World Events 1950

February	Moscow	Stalin and Mao formed an alliance of the USSR and China.
April	Amman	King Abdullah of Jordan annexed Arab Palestine to create an expanded Kingdom of Jordan incorporating the territory captured by the Arab Legion in the war with Israel.
June	Korea	Communist North Korea invaded independent South Korea leading to United Nations intervention and the Korean War.
October	Lebanon	The pipeline linking Dhahran to Sidon (Trans-Arabian Pipeline) was completed.
October	Tibet	Chinese troops invaded Tibet.
November	Libya	United Nations granted independence to Libya.
November	Cairo	King Farouk demanded total and immediate evacuation of British troops from the Suez Canal Zone.

Notes

1 The reference to slave traffic was later deleted.
2 Now the Ministry of Defence (Army).

3 Major 'Mike' Hankin-Turvin was seconded from the Arab Legion in Jordan on the recommendation of General Glubb Pasha, the Commander of the Arab Legion, who also selected the Arab officers and other ranks.
4 *Chandal* poles are hard mangrove poles imported from India and were used extensively in the Gulf for building (see Plates 28 and 33).
5 Later to be known as the Qasimia.

3

1951

January

The Trucial Oman Levies (TOL) were formally established by King's Regulation No 1 of 1951 under Article 82 of the Trucial States Order in Council 1950. This document was signed by Sir Rupert Hay, Her Majesty's Political Resident in the Persian Gulf and Mr Ernest Bevin, the Foreign Secretary.

The Trucial Oman Levies Regulation laid down their tasks as:

> the maintenance of peace and good order in the Trucial States
> providing an escort for the British Political Representatives.

The terms of enlistment for local Arab other rank recruits were for a two-year contract with 14 days leave per year. The rates of pay were to start at a basic Rupees 60/= per month and are shown in detail on page 165 (the Indian rupee was then worth 1*s.* 6*d.*).

The TOL advance party was not expected to leave Jordan for Sharjah before 20 January 1951. The equipment and stores from the UK were due to arrive off Dubai on the SS *Turkistan* on 14 February and the main detachment from Jordan sometime later. The advance party arrived before the end of the month and started to recruit local administrative personnel.

February

On 19 February 1951, the Political Resident issued a directive that the TOL were not to:

> (1) go south of Latitude 24 degrees 20 minutes North, except on specific instruction of the Political Officer Trucial States or in hot pursuit;[1]
> (2) enter Muscat territory, ie Musandam east of the line joining

> Dibba to Sha'am north-west of Ras al Khaima, and all country south of Latitude 24 degrees 50 minutes North and East of Longitude 56 East[2] but may operate in the Wadi Qaur up to the Muscat boundary.[3]

On 26 February 1951, the Foreign Office informed the Political Resident in Bahrain that it would like to include the Buraimi Oasis in the areas to which the TOL were not to go. It is not recorded if this request was in fact granted by the PR.

On 27 February 1951, the main body of men arrived from Jordan. It is unlikely that they flew direct from Amman to Sharjah. The 'routine Dakota flight' could have carried them from Amman to the RAF base at Habbaniyah were it stopped for the night. The next day they would have landed at the RAF base at Magil near Basra, had their lunch at RAF Bahrain, arriving at RAF Sharjah in the afternoon.

On 28 February, the first nine locally enlisted drivers signed on, they included Drivers Mohammed Saleh (84), Yousef Eid, Said Salim al Si'ar (107), Ali al Iraqi and Hassan Ali Akhu Noora.

March

The first ten days after the arrival of the main body was spent by all available personnel shovelling sand out of their buildings in the Levies Camp and carting it away.

Catering for the Arab ranks of the whole unit was by outside contract as was the laundry. It is most likely that the contractor for both these services was Isa Mousa Isa of Sharjah. Likewise, the 'wet' and 'dry' sweepers employed in the Levies Camp may have been under their leader, Ali Gumbar, from these early days.[4]

The first 'operation' recorded for the TOL was a visit on 15 March 1951 to Shaikh Said bin Maktoum, the Ruler of Dubai. The following day there was a visit to the acting Ruler of Sharjah, Shaikh Mohammed bin Saqr, the Ruler's brother. The Ruler was in London for medical treatment.

On 17 March, they visited Ras al Khaima and were away for two nights getting to Al Sha'am, Rams, Falaj al Ain and calling upon Shaikh Ali bin Saif of the Khawatir and Shaikh Mohammed bin Ali Huwaidim of the Beni Qitab.

The report continues that, on 24 March, they went to Kalba to visit Shaikh Hamed and on to Fujairah and Khor Fakkan and ends with the comment that no visit was made to Abu Dhabi as the Ruler, Shaikh Shakhbut bin Sultan, was away hunting.

The Ruler of Sharjah, Shaikh Sultan bin Saqr al Qasimi, died in London on 23 March 1951. His body was returned to Sharjah for burial. The TOL provided a Guard of Honour at his funeral.[5]

The PDTC first exploratory well at Ras Sadr in Abu Dhabi Shaikhdom was abandoned at 13,000 feet (4,000 metres).

Also, during March, the recognition of the status of Fujairah was the subject of much discussion.

April

From the British Agency in Sharjah, located on the creekside at Mujarrah, Mr Wilton, the Political Agent, reported on 4 April 1951 that the TOL had been established for one month in the Levy Lines at the RAF Station Sharjah and that Major Hankin-Turvin, two Arab officers, 10 non-commissioned officers and 22 men from the Arab Legion had arrived on 27 February, 9 drivers and 9 cooks and others had been recruited locally so, as at 31 March, a total of 53, all ranks, were present. The Jordanian personnel were mainly tradesmen and specialists and included Technical Storeman Toma Attallah and Vehicle Mechanic Emil Gosoos.

May

During May 1951, the first nine local 'fighting men' were enlisted. These included Jundis Mohammed Nakhaira bin Mahroum (143), Nakhaira Mohammed Neyadi, Salimeen Salim, Miftah Abdullah, Rashid Mubarak Hiyali and Khalifa Salem bin Kharsoom. They completed two months' training in Sharjah under a Jordanian Corporal Ali before being deployed to outstations. Jundi Mohammed Nakhaira went to the Wadi Qaur where the post strength was 15 all ranks.

The soldiers' dress was similar to that of the Jordanian Arab Legion Desert Police (the Badia) consisting of a long khaki cloak (*thaub*) worn over white trousers; the red *shmagh* and *'agal* without any badge; a leather waist bandolier with crossed shoulder straps. The single silver *khanjar* badge of the TOL was devised at about this time and made by the silversmith in Sharjah *suq*. It was worn by the locally enlisted troops whilst the Arab legionnaires most likely wore their own badge during their attachment to the TOL.

Two officers and one sergeant of the Arab Legion were returned to Jordan for disciplinary reasons and were quickly replaced.

The Political Agent reported to Bahrain that 'Bin Qatami, an alleged slave trader, was pursued to Dhank by a patrol of the TOL on the 31st' but did not record his capture.

June

At 0600 hours on 2 June 1951, a TOL column consisting of the Commandant and 25 other ranks, in two Bedfords and four Land-rovers, left base travelling south over the Ramlet al Faya and Ramlet Anej to the Buraimi Oasis, Hafit, Qabil and Dhank. They met Shaikh Zayed bin Sultan al Nahyan[6] and discussed the activities of slave traders in the village of Buraimi with Shaikh Saqr bin Sultan al Na'imi.[7] The column returned to Sharjah at 1700 hours on 8 June. This would indicate that the Foreign Office had been persuaded that patrols into these areas were necessary at the Commandant's discretion.

July

The Ruler of Kalba, Shaikh Hamed, was assassinated by Saqr bin Sultan bin Salim who took over the territory. Sultan bin Salim, his father the ex-Ruler of Ras al Khaima, had his stronghold in Howailat and hence control of the Wadi Qaur, which was the main route through the mountains to the Batina. The Political Officer Trucial Coast and Major Hankin-Turvin with some TOL went to Kalba to investigate the situation.

Some of the local Levies were brought back from the Wadi Qaur post to Sharjah to take their part in patrol duties.

August

The Arbitration Meeting between the Ruler of Abu Dhabi and the Iraq Petroleum Company (parent of PDTC) took place in Paris at the end of August 1951. Shaikh Shakhbut and Shaikh Zayed attended the meeting to resolve the terms of their oil concession.

Among those from the Arab Legion recommended on 20 August for a second year of duty with the TOL was Technical Storeman 27901 Thoma Attallah.

September

Shaikh Rashid bin Hamed Al Shamisi of Hamasa in the Buraimi Oasis, was reported to have raised the Saudi flag over his village, whilst Shaikh Mohammed bin Salimeen of the *bedu* section of the Al Bu Shamis around Qabil to the south, declared his allegiance to the Ruler of Abu Dhabi.

At this period the TOL received orders not to operate west of a line running due south from Mirfa. A Saudi tax collector with armed guards was reported to be active in the Bainuna, Liwa, al Batin and Dhafra areas.

Major Hankin-Turvin requested the supply of two three-inch mortars in a message dated September 1951.[8] It sould seem that he foresaw the need for a major increase in their potential firepower, more in terms of 'bang' than actual lethality, should his very small deployable response force be faced with vastly superior numbers of recalcitrant tribesmen armed with the modern rifles then becoming available to them. The two-inch mortars had insufficient range for use in open desert and were quite ineffective. Among the Arab Legion ranks there would have been trained three-inch mortarmen.

October

The Aden Protectorate Levies (APL) were approached with a request for instructors to replace those from the Arab Legion whose contracts would run out at the end of the year.[9]

The TOL strength was 1 British officer, 30 Jordanians and 50 local other ranks.

November

The Saudi Government stepped up their frontier claims during November 1951 and the British Government replied that they had never recognised any Saudi claim beyond the line prepared in 1938. It was anticipated that the conference between the two Governments on the boundaries with Qatar and the Trucial Shaikhdoms would take place in January 1952.

This strain in the relations between UK and Saudi Arabia caused the latter to request the winding up by the end of 1951 of the British Military Mission to the Kingdom of Saudi Arabia under Brigadier Baird, who was training the Saudi National Guard at Taif.[10] Among the British officers of the Military Mission were Majors Martin and

Smith, Captains Warner and Rowcliffe and Warrant Officer Barnes, all of whom served later with the TOL.

December

The December 1951 Progress Report No 1 on the TOL stated that of the 50 local recruits to date, 30 were *bedu* and estimated that by 1 December 1952 all general duty personnel up to and including the rank of *areef* (corporal) would be locally enlisted.

The Arab Legion detachment were largely replaced by fresh volunteers from Jordan.

World Events 1951

January	Taif	The Arabian American Oil Company (ARAMCO) agreed to share profits with the Saudi Arabian Government.
March	Teheran	The Iranian Parliament voted to nationalise the Anglo Iranian Oil Company. The Abadan refinery closed on 15 April.
July	Jerusalem	King Abdullah of Jordan was shot dead outside the Mosque of Omar. He had ruled Jordan for thirty years. His younger son Emir Naif was proclaimed Regent as the Crown Prince Talal was in Beirut for treatment for mental illness.
September	Iran	Iranian troops seized the oil refinery at Abadan.
October	Suez	British troops took control of all key points on the Canal and in the Canal Zone.
November	Syria	Colonel Adeeb Shishakly overthrew the Government.
December	Libya	King Idriss el Senussi proclaimed the independence of Libya.

Notes

1 This is roughly a line from just south of Mafraq Abu Dhabi in the west to Mahadha in the east.

2 These lines intersect near the Hadhf neutral zone to the north of Mahadha.

3 Wadi Qaur was the main route between Sharjah and the Batina and Muscat; the Muscat border post was at Aswad.

4 These terms were inherited from India, the 'wet' sweeper attending to the latrines and the 'dry' sweeper to all other cleaning and sweeping duties.

5 The acting Ruler, his brother Shaikh Mohammed bin Saqr, succeeded him. However, Shaikh Sultan's son, Saqr, claimed that 'sons of age and ability to succeed would normally do so'. Shaikh Mohammed later acknowledged this claim and resigned in favour of his nephew Shaikh Saqr bin Sultan al Qasimi.

6 Shaikh Zayed bin Sultan al Nahyan, the youngest brother of the Ruler of Abu Dhabi Shaikh Shakhbut, was his Representative in the Eastern Region (to use the modern equivalent). Shaikh Zayed lived in the fort at Al Muwaqi and was responsible for the six Abu Dhabi villages in the Buraimi Oasis. These are Al Ain, Mua'taradh, Al Muwaqi, Jimi, Qatara and Hili. In August 1966, Shaikh Zayed became Ruler of Abu Dhabi and has been the President of the United Arab Emirates since it was formed on 2 December 1971.

7 The villages of Hamasa, Sa'ara and Buraimi itself nominally owed allegiance to the Sultan of Muscat and Oman through the paramount Shaikh of the Na'im, Shaikh Saqr bin Sultan of Buraimi.

8 Three-inch mortars were received in July 1958.

9 Since before the Second World War, locally recruited ground forces in Iraq and the Aden Protectorate had as their main role the defence and security of the RAF bases in those territories. Air power was the means used to control desert and mountain areas, hence the responsibility for all 'military' units and operations lay with the RAF. They provided the HQ, command and logistic structure and officered and supported the local Levies ground units with RAF Regiment personnel in addition to the presence of RAF Regiment units. The Arab Legion in Jordan, on the other hand, had always been the responsibility of the British Army. When it became apparent that the Arab Legion were not going to be able to continue to provide specialised manpower for the TOL for much longer, the choice lay between the Iraq Levies in Habbaniyah, who were recruited from Assyrians and Kurds, and the Aden Protectorate Levies, recruited from the southern Arabian tribes. Another factor was that the Persian Gulf came under the command of the Commander-in-Chief in Aden.

10 Brigadier J E A Baird CBE (Robert) was a member of the Intelligence Staff of the 8th Army during the Western Desert campaigns of the Second World War. As a fluent Arabic speaker, he was head of the British Military Mission, training the Saudi Arabian National Guard in Taif for a number of years. Recalled to British Forces Middle East Headquarters at the end of 1951, he was sent as adviser to the Political Resident in Bahrain until becoming Senior Army Officer Persian Gulf (SAOPG) in due course.

4

1952

January
Brigadier Baird visited Bahrain, Kuwait, Qatar and Sharjah from the British HQ Middle East Land Forces in the Suez Canal Zone.

Shaikh Obaid bin Juma'a of the Bani Ka'ab and Shaikh Said bin Rashid al Baluchi of Ma'azam visited Saudi Arabia probably on travel documents provided by Shaikh Rashid bin Hamed al Shamisi of Hamasa.

February
The conference held in Dammam to discuss the Saudi Arabian border claims against Abu Dhabi and Qatar failed to achieve any results.

The Saudi official, Ibn Mansur, and a party of tax collectors made their base at Agaila in the Bainuna.

The TOL set up a post at the western end of the Wadi Qaur which they believed to be in Sharjah territory. About 30 Bani Ka'ab tribesmen mounted an attack on the post and a few shots were exchanged before a parley was arranged. It was discovered that the post was on Bani Ka'ab land. Three of the Bani Ka'ab then asked to join the TOL.

Jundi Hassan Abdullah Noman (152) joined and was employed as a clerk in the Orderly Room. Mr Nayer was a civilian Orderly-Room clerk. Mr Menon was in charge of the Signal Office.

The working dress was khaki drill shirt and trousers. Fatigues and other dirty work was done in denims.

Shaikh Khalid bin Ahmed, the ex-Regent of Kalba, formally ceded Dhaid to the Ruler of Sharjah.

March

General Sir Brian Robertson, the Commander-in-Chief Middle East Land Forces, visited Sharjah and inspected the TOL on 14 March.

The force was now up to strength but the manning of the post in Wadi Qaur had left only a small reserve available in Sharjah. It was planned to set up a further post at Jabal al Faya and to organise camel patrols from the Bani Qitab operating from Tawi Fili under orders of, and in co-operation with, the TOL.

The Ruler of Ras al Khaima with about 100 of his men attacked Rams by night and recaptured the village. Soon after this, the Ruler of Ras al Khaima, accompanied by a TOL patrol, visited Sha'am.

The Royal Navy frigate, HMS *Wren*, anchored off Kalba and RAF Vampire aircraft flew reconnaisance sorties over Kalba to put pressure upon Saqr bin Sultan. The TOL obtained authority to cross Muscat territory in the Aswad area on their way to Kalba.

On 24 March, Fujairah, under the leadership of Shaikh Mohammed bin Hamad al Sharqi, was formally recognised as the seventh of the Trucial Shaikhdoms.

April

The Political Resident, Sir Rupert Hay, with a TOL escort, went on a tour to Wadi Hatta as far as Wajajah where the track became impassable for motor vehicles. He returned to drive along the Wadi Qaur to Howailat and visited Dhaid, Ras al Khaima and Umm al Quwain. Shaikh Mohammed bin Salim, the brother of the Ruler of Ras al Khaima, told the PR that 'the TOL posts at Kharus and Wadi Qaur and their Bani Qitab camel patrols at Tawi Fili had made a great improvement in the local situation and that the TOL presence was much appreciated'.

May

On 13 May, the usurper Saqr bin Sultan withdrew from Kalba to Murair in Muscat territory, and the Ruler of Sharjah regained possession of the town accompanied by Major Hankin-Turvin with the TOL in support.

Shaikh Saqr bin Sultan al Na'imi of Buraimi village threatened to go to Saudi Arabia if he was not granted petroleum exploration concessions.

June (Ramadan)
Brigadier Baird was again in the Gulf, this time visiting Qatar with the PR. His appointment as military adviser to the PR probably came about at this time.

July
Saudi Government employees were reported to have visited the PDTC camp at Tarif.

Rumours were circulating in Bahrain and in the Trucial Coast of the Saudi Arabian intention to send a representative to Buraimi and the Dhahira.

A TOL patrol went to the Dhaid area on information that an ambush had been laid for the ruler of Sharjah who was due to pass that way. The ambush party had left by the time the patrol reached the area.

During 13 and 14 July, an attempt was made to recapture Rams by some of those who had fled earlier supported by some of the Shihuh.[1] A TOL detachment was sent to Rams and the Royal Navy cruiser HMS *Flamingo* landed about 50 men to assist but the attempt failed. The naval party re-embarked and the TOL established a post of ten men with a Bren gun in a tower near Rams.

Jundi Said Abdullah Noman was enlisted as an armourer.

Three camels were stolen from the Bani Qitab by an 'Amiri tribesman.

August
The Saudi tax-collecting party at Agaila were also reported to be covering the Jabal Dhanna area.

The TOL recovered the three stolen Bani Qitab camels and a TOL patrol visited Kalba and Fujairah.

On 31 August, the Saudi official Turki bin Ataishan, previously the Governor of Ras Tanura, arrived in Hamasa with a number of cars and trucks. He brought a wireless station and was accompanied by not less than 30 men including armed retainers. He was welcomed by the Al Bu Shamis shaikhs and proclaimed that he had come as the Governor of the region, appointed by the Saudi Arabian Government.

September

Thirty TOL were sent to Al Ain, and RAF Vampires at Sharjah made flights over the Buraimi Oasis in response to the Saudi incursion. It is likely that the TOL detachment was based at the Murabb'a Zayed as it was outside any villages with easy access to the water supply of the Sarouj *falaj*, in addition to providing a vantage point for observation.

Major Hankin-Turvin was recalled from leave in mid-September.

Three soldiers of the TOL of the Al Bu Shamis deserted to Turki bin Ataishan in Hamasa. Their rifles were later returned by the Saudis to the TOL.

October

TOL recruit serial numbers had reached 175 (Ali Azaiz bin Maktoum). Their training in Sharjah was under Corporal Majid Saleh of the Arab Legion and lasted for a long six and a half months.

Sixty men were reported as having been sent to support Shaikh Saqr al Na'imi in Buraimi. These must have been *wali's askaris* sent on the orders of the Sultan of Muscat.[2]

The Sultan of Muscat assembled a tribal force in Sohar with the intention of ejecting the Saudi party from Hamasa but was dissuaded from deploying it through the Wadi Jizzi by the British Government. The British Consul in Muscat, Mr Chauncy, drove from Muscat to deliver these instructions. He travelled in great haste along the beach and through the palm gardens of the Batina and arrived just in time. It is interesting to speculate how matters would have developed had his vehicle broken down.[3]

A 'Stand-Still' Agreement on the Buraimi dispute was reached on 26 October 1953 between the British and Saudi Arabian Governments. Both sides were to refrain from taking actions that would affect the situation existing at that time. This meant no further subversion by bribes or political activity and no additional military activity.

November

A PDTC seismic survey party was now operating in the area south of Al Khatt.

On 10 November, the PR was escorted by Major Hankin-Turvin, with a patrol of the TOL, on a visit to Muscat through the Wadi Qaur.

The Buraimi Stand-Still Agreement was not being complied with by the Saudis. Turki bin Ataishan sent his car to Qattara and 'seduced' a number of the inhabitants, according to the Political Agency report.[4] In addition, Turki had sent cars to fetch Sulaiman bin Himyar from his village of Tanuf in central Oman and to carry him on to Riyadh, whence he returned later in the month.[5]

Major Colin Maxwell, the newly appointed commander of the proposed Batinah Force of the Muscat Armed Forces, arrived in Sohar where the force was to have its base.

December

The TOL post at Mugattarah was withdrawn as the Saudis were now using a route some 50 kilometres to the south, outside the undisputed territory, for their traffic to Buraimi.

The Abu Dhabi *wali* at Markhiya in the Bainuna was forced to leave his post with his men by the Saudi tax collector. Shaikh Said bin Shakhbut re-established the post with 75 men and 25 of Shaikh Shakhbut's men were also sent to set up a post in the Liwa.[6]

Shaikh Mohammed bin Ali of the Bani Qitab went to Riyadh. It is not recorded whether he travelled by Saudi vehicle from Hamasa but this would have been most likely.

A confrontation between the Bani Ka'ab followers of Obaid bin Juma and the Muqabil in the Wadi Jizzi ended peacefully without TOL intervention as it was outside their area of responsibility.

Five ex-members of the APL had been recruited as lance corporals for the TOL and the force was to be expanded to 130 all ranks.

World Events 1952

January	Cairo	Anti-British riots kill 17 and burn the Turf Club and Shepheard's Hotel.
July	Cairo	General Mohammed Neguib seizes power in a military coup. King Farouk abdicates in favour of his nine-month-old son.
August	Amman	Crown Prince Hussain bin Talal crowned King of Jordan as his father was suffering incurable mental illness.
October	Kenya	British troops sent to quell Mau-Mau terrorism. Jomo Kenyatta arrested.
November	USA	General Eisenhower succeeds Harry Truman as President.

Notes

1 The Shihuh of the Musandam peninsula are a composite tribe cultivating small, mountain-terrace fields during the winter when rainfall can be collected in underground cisterns. In summer, they move down to date gardens in their coastal settlements around the peninsula near Ras al Khaima and Dibba. They are known for their small axe-like weapons and their shrill whistles when communicating from hill to hill.

2 The Government of Muscat and Oman appointed local Governors, or *walis*, to each of their internal districts based in the major villages. Each *wali* had an un-uniformed group of armed men to enforce law and keep order and provide guards. Generally known as *Wali's askaris*, they acted as an untrained gendarmerie.

3 The Sultan Sayid Said bin Taymour was at Sohar when Mr Chauncy arrived and made him read the British Government's message to the assembled leaders.

4 This presumably refers to a meeting with the Darmaki family who lived in Qattara.

5 Sulaiman bin Himyar, paramount Shaikh of the Bani Riyam.

6 Shaikh Said bin Shakhbut, the Ruler of Abu Dhabi's eldest son.

5

1953

January

The Governor of Aden agreed that up to 400 men of the APL could be available for duty for six months in the Trucial States. This was soon changed to a total of 300 men who might be divided 200 to the TOL and 100 to the oil-company funded 'Huqf Force', which was later to land there at Ras Duqm as the Muscat Field Force (MFF).

The Saudi Turki bin Ataishan and Shaikh Rashid bin Hamed al Shamisi visited Mahadha.

Four trucks with some 100 tribesmen, including Shaikh Mohammed bin Ali the paramount Shaikh of the Bani Qitab, arrived in Hamasa from Riyadh on 14 January. This large number of presumably armed men, who would be returning to their tribal area, indicated the nature and extent of the Saudi intentions.

Operation Boxer

On 21 January, Operation Boxer took place. This was the landing over the beach at Jabal Ali of a mobile squadron of the RAF Regiment, consisting of one flight with twelve Humber armoured cars and one reconnaisance flight with their Landrovers, in all about 100 men.[1] They drove at once to the RAF lines in Sharjah. They had come from the RAF base in Habbaniya (Iraq), overland to Basra, thence in the LST *Evan Gibb*.

Also part of the operation, simultaneously, No 6 Squadron RAF of twelve Vampire fighter ground attack aircraft landed at RAF Sharjah and the Royal Navy cruiser HMS *Ceylon* arrived off Sharjah for her routine annual visit.

The directive for Operation Boxer stated that 'the force was entering the territory by agreement with the Rulers to strengthen the power of the rulers to protect their territory. The force was not to take hostile action against the people of Saudi Arabia but to assist in repelling attack on the undisputed territories (of the Trucial States) and to prevent passage of undesirable persons through such territories'.

Two days later, on 23 January, the small TOL post at the western approaches to the Wadi Qaur was surrounded by some 50 Bani Ka'ab tribesmen under Shaikh Abdullah bin Salim, who arrived 'flying a Saudi flag' and demanded their surrender. The TOL corporal in charge of the post insisted that he was unable to do this without authority and obtained a truce until he was able to get a lift back to Sharjah on a passing civilian 'taxi' to report.

At 0220 hrs on 24 January, a combined force under Major Hankin-Turvin left Sharjah by the Jabal Faya route to the Wadi Qaur. The force consisted of 39 Levies with rifles, three Bren guns and one two-inch mortar in three Landrovers and one Bedford, plus three Humber armoured cars and seven Landrovers with seven Bren guns manned by the RAF Regiment. The 12 Vampire aircraft stood by in support. Two of the armoured cars were held up in the dunes but arrived in the Wadi Qaur later that day.

At dawn, 0700 hrs, the column arrived at the entrance to the Wadi Qaur. Twenty-four tribesmen were seen in positions to the north of and overlooking the track, others were on the high ground to the south. The TOL and RAF Regiment troops dismounted and took up positions at some 500 metres from them.

Rais (Captain) Nasr el Nil (Arab Legion attached TOL) went forward to parley. By then four Vampire aircraft were overhead. After some time Shaikh Abdullah bin Salim was located and agreed to withdraw his men. The column then continued on to the TOL post where the three Levies were still manning their slit trenches.

A piece of cloth bearing a design of palm trees, camels and crossed swords and bearing the words 'Long live the Saudi Arabian Kingdom' was found to be flying, upside down, over Shaikh Abdullah bin Salim's camp and was confiscated. No shot was fired throughout the operation.

The TOL troop of 30 men remained in the area and the rest of the force returned to Sharjah on 25 January.

The Abu Dhabi causeway was completed by PDTC and drilling

planned to start at Tarif. The rig at Ras Sadr was dismantled and the PDTC operation at Jabal Ali was closing down.

In Hamasa, two houses were being built under Saudi auspices. These were probably Bait Turki[2] and Bait Aqeel.[3] Two Syrian doctors arrived to join Turki from Saudi Arabia and 'Ibn Mahdi', a Saudi official, was expected to arrive in Hamasa.

February

The Vampires of No 6 Squadron RAF left Sharjah on 18 February having completed their part in Operation Boxer. The Humber armoured cars and Landrovers of the RAF Regiment carried out patrols in the undisputed territory of the Trucial States.

In Hamasa, the Saudis were issuing rice to women and children from all the villages around Buraimi in contravention of the Stand-Still Agreement.

At Murban (Tarif), the drill struck salt water but carried on working.

A contingent of 208 APL arrived in Sharjah and took over the TOL posts in the Wadi Qaur and Tawi Salim just north of the Ramlet Anej. This contingent is likely to have been made up of one rifle squadron and a small headquarter element under command of their own British RAF Regiment officers and Arab APL *mulazims* and NCOs. Their sub units were not deployed into the disputed Buraimi zone but freed the TOL from many duties in the undisputed areas. This allowed the TOL to resume training in addition to their presence in Buraimi within the terms of the Stand-still Agreement.

With the arrival of the APL, the contract catering arrangements ended and the unit's own cookhouse was set up using the 'Number 1 Field Cooking Sets' that the APL had brought with them. Similar equipment was still in use in 1960.

The TOL strength had reached 110.

In Sohar, the Batinah Force was now 25 strong with four ex-APL NCOs. Major Maxwell had been joined by Major St John Armitage.

Shaikh Abdullah bin Salim al Ka'abi changed his allegiance to Shaikh Zayed bin Sultan in Al Ain and asked for a TOL post to be put at Sharm.[4]

The following were to be recruited in Aden from among the APL and ex-APL personnel for the TOL:

4 x officers (later amended)
1 x regimental quartermaster sergeant
1 x company sergeant major
6 x sergeants (4 x GD, 1 x armourer, 1 x stores)
12 x corporals (1 x English/Arabic typist, 1 x signaller)
126 x privates (30 potential drivers, 30 potential signallers, 3 x fitters, 3 x clerks, 3 x storemen)

March

From Hamasa, Turki sent money to Obaid bin Juma in Khatwa in the Wadi Jizzi to help him against his rival Shaikh Abdulla bin Salim of the Bani Ka'ab.

Ibn Mansur, the Saudi tax collector, appeared at Tarif with four vehicles and 38 armed men and went on to Hamasa and Buraimi by another route. He then toured to the south and west and returned to Saudi Arabia through Tarif.

The PDTC seismic party from Al Khatt moved to Dhaid.

The second contingent of the APL arrived from Aden together with their vehicles making their total strength about 300. This contingent was the second rifle squadron to arrive.

RAF Meteor aircraft were now based in Sharjah for reconnaisance.

The TOL was now 145 strong and a patrol visited Sharm to support Abdullah bin Salim.

Major W J Martin, Suffolk Regiment, joined the TOL to take over command of the enlarged force.

A new establishment for the TOL was agreed and its planned new organisation is outlined in Appendix 12 (page 167).

The recruitment policy was that emphasis would not be on enlisting local Arabs as their tribal loyalties might conflict with their military duties. Accordingly, two squadrons were to be recruited from the Aden Protectorate and one from the Trucial Coast mainly from the shaikhdom of Abu Dhabi.

The RSM was WO1 Daud Sidqi al Nobbisi and the Chief Clerk was WO2 Zaki Shwaihat, both from the Arab Legion.

The Ration Scales for the Force were based on those used by the APL. The Arab-Legion style of dress had long been replaced by British Army tropical khaki drill trousers and shirts. Brass TOL shoulder titles had been designed and were to be ordered from British Army suppliers. The silver single *khanjar* brooch-type badges for the *'agal* continued to be made in the Sharjah *suq* and the silver crossed *khanjars* badge for the British officers' headdress were also made there with two lugs and a split pin for their khaki service dress peaked caps (see Plate 1).

April

Major W J Martin was promoted to Lieutenant-colonel as commander designate of the Trucial Oman Levies. He had previously served with Brigadier Baird in the British Military Mission as Training Officer with the Saudi National Guard in Taif.

It was found that Aden could not provide Arab officers of the right calibre and experience so three more British officers of the rank of captain were requested.

The TOL HQ was located within the RAF compound to the rear of the BOAC Fort building and close to the HQ offices of the RAF Station. The troops lived in the old Levies Camp, also within the RAF compound, but at the far end with their own parade ground and guard-room on the eastern side of the compound. The British officers and NCOs lived in their RAF equivalent Mess.

The continuing contraventions of the Buraimi Stand-still Agreement by the Saudis caused the British Government to respond by deploying detachments of the TOL to Agaila, Jabal Dhanna, Iqlat al Nakhala and by increasing the Buraimi garrison to place Hamasa under a loose blockade.

The squadron in Buraimi, which had its base at Murabb'a Zayed set up posts at:

Post 1: Qattara – beside Bait Darumki (under command of Corporal Mohammed Nakhira)
Post 2: Burj bin Hilal at Jimi
Post 3: Ghafat Shahine – south of the *wadi*
Post 4: Nedd al Gharban – south of the Hamasa tower
Post 5: In the Buraimi-Sa'ara gap

It also laid night ambushes in positions north of Hamasa.

Also taking part in the blockade, the Wali of Buraimi's *askaris* held a post near the Qasr al Khandaq. They were, of course, independent of Shaikh Saqr al Nai'mi of Buraimi village.

The palm gardens of Hamasa and Buraimi run together so it was not possible to isolate Hamasa from Buraimi for the purposes of the blockade. The open country to the south, west and north of the two villages were therefore covered by four of the TOL posts. The fifth was in the corridor between Buraimi village and Sa'ara date gardens. Shaikh Saqr had undertaken to maintain the blockade in the east and south-eastern sector where his village lay. To the south of Buraimi village is the Qasr al Khandaq, the large fort of Buraimi, which was also held by Shaikh Saqr. The Wali of Buraimi had been out-manoeuvred by Shaikh Saqr and his small number of men relegated to a minor role in the blockade ring. It became increasingly evident that, whereas by day the blockade seemed to be effective, by night there was considerable coming and going between Buraimi and Hamasa.

A Saudi car carrying three Saudis and five Omanis, returning to Hamasa from central Oman, was stopped by one of these posts. The party was ordered to leave the territory and directed on to Salwa, as the nearest location in Saudi Arabia by road, but their car broke down and they had to be repatriated by sea.

On 23 April, the TOL missed capturing a party of slaves who were being embarked on a *dhow* on the coast between Dubai and Sharjah. Documents found in the car being used implicated Khalifa bin Majid, the cousin of the Ruler of Dubai.

The PDTC seismic party completed their work in the area of Dhaid and moved to Jabal Dhanna.

May

A further six British officers had now arrived together with some British NCOs. They were appointed as follows:

OC HQ Squadron	Captain D Shaw, Royal Artillery
Quartermaster	Captain T Rowcliffe, The Buffs
Adjutant (later MTO)	Captain A R Steggles, Royal Artillery
Paymaster	Sergeant Wilcox, Royal Army Pay Corps
	Sergeant S Chinn, Royal Electrical and Mechanical Engineers
	Corporal W Cruickshank, Royal Electrical and Mechanical Engineers
OC A Squadron (Buraimi)	Major P MacDonald, Border Regiment
OC B Squadron (Tarif)	Major H O D Thwaites MC, 9th Lancers

OC Training (Sharjah)	Captain C W Criddle, Somerset Light Infantry

The additional pay granted to seconded British personnel is shown in Appendix 13 on page 170.

The APL post at Jabal Dhanna was withdrawn as it was serving no useful purpose there. A TOL post was put at Bada Suwailim, some 30 kilometres south of Agaila, and another TOL post was being established at Arada in the Liwa to prevent possible Saudi infiltration.[5] A 'tribal post' manned by the Ruler of Abu Dhabi's men was set up further west at Suwaitiyah.

In Sharjah, about 150 recruits from Aden arrived and the APL took over the RAF Regiment armoured cars, as most of the British personnel had now been withdrawn. The reported strength of the TOL was 367, of whom 258 were in Sharjah. The APL were 323 in number of whom 176 were in Sharjah.

During the month, a caravan of 24 camels was known to have reached the Saudis in Hamasa.

Shaikh Zayed's men attacked and captured the post at Mazyad from Ahmed bin Salf al Khawatir of Hafit.

June

The expansion of the TOL was proceeding and the APL were expected to be able to return to Aden in July leaving a few specialists for training. The first order for brass TOL shoulder titles was placed for 700 sets (see Plate 32).

Mr Christopher Pirie-Gordon took over as the Political Agent, Trucial Coast, in the new British Agency building on the Dubai creekside.

The Bani Ka'ab under Obaid bin Juma were interfering with the traffic to Buraimi and fired upon the Political Officer, Mr Martin Buckmaster. The TOL post at Sharm was also fired upon so action was taken and the TOL cleared and occupied Burj Obaid near Mahadha.

General Headquarters Middle East Land Forces (GHQMELF) reported to the War Office in London their estimate that by the end of July the TOL would be able to take over operational duties from the APL who would then return to Aden. A small Land Forces HQ would be set up in Bahrain under Brigadier Baird to take over local command of land forces from the RAF. The staff was to be two officers and ten other ranks. This became known as Headquarters Local Land Forces Persian Gulf (HQLLFPG) and Brigadier Baird as the Senior Army Officer Persian Gulf (SAOPG). The TOL came under their command.

Though Aden and Iraq continued to be under RAF command, the TOL as the only land force unit in the Gulf was an Army unit. It was appropriate to form an Army command as the takeover of all internal security responsibility in the Middle East Command from the RAF by the Army was under discussion at that time.

July

Captain Steggles, RSM Daud Sidqi and about eight men were flown in an Anson aircraft into Arada airstrip in the western end of the Liwa. Their task was to move that post to Humar and there to lay out another airstrip. It took them about three weeks to complete the task in midsummer using camels for transport. The Humar Post was left under command of Mulazim Abdullah Hussain who had served his time with the APL camel patrols.

Captain Steggles, RSM Daud and six men with a local guide travelled by camel the length of the Liwa to Al Khis where there was another small TOL post with a radio station. From here they set out for Buraimi and were out of radio contact for the week it took them to reach the squadron HQ in Murabba' Zayed. This was a remarkable exploit even for the local *bedu* who would have avoided travelling these distances by camel in midsummer.

The TOL set up their own medical casualty reception station (CRS) in Sharjah and started to train six Arab medical orderlies under the RAF Medical Officer.

The recruits from Aden, said to be trained one-time APL soldiers who were to form C Squadron, arrived in Sharjah and were enlisted and issued with their equipment.

The argument in London between the Foreign Office and the War Office over the responsibility for funding the TOL was still continuing and directly affecting many decisions concerning the unit.

The PDTC party at Ras al Akhdhar that was working in the area up towards the Qatar border was being guarded by a detachment of 15 TOL.

August

On 3 August, Major Hankin-Turvin completed the hand-over of the unit to Lieutenant-Colonel Martin and left the TOL.

The Hamasa blockade succeeded in intercepting several camel trains.

Major MacDonald took the new Adeni draft that was to become C Squadron from Sharjah to Buraimi pending the arrival of Major Thwaites.

Captain R Warner, Duke of Wellington's Regiment, had joined the TOL and took over B Squadron at Maghaira from Major Thwaites who went to Buraimi to take over the new C Squadron. Major MacDonald returned to Sharjah and A Squadron.

Captain Steggles and his party arrived from the Liwa and returned to Sharjah by truck. He was then appointed Motor Transport Officer and was joined by Artificer Sergeant Playfor, Royal Artillery, as MT Sergeant.

Morris trucks 4 x 4 GS 1 ton arrived for use as section vehicles together with a number of Morris 4 x 4 water trucks and a few Austin trucks 4 x 4 GS 1 ton. These vehicles were standard British Army vehicles with the standard, narrow high-pressure track-grip tyres used in north-west Europe.

Until many years later these Morris trucks remained in their dark green paint, as there were more important things to be done, but it did make them unduly hot to touch in summer. Only the cab roofs were painted with white quarters for recognition from the air (see Plate 4).

They gave the unit mobility down to section level but were severely limited in their cross-country capability due to their unsuitable tyres and lack of power in high-ambient temperatures. They were not fitted with efficient fuel filters and suffered badly as the petrol in the outstations was frequently contaminated with water and dust. Their narrow track and high centre of gravity made them easy to turn over on the deeply rutted tracks in the sandy areas. The water trucks were dangerous when partly filled and the water could build up enough oscillation to cause the driver to lose control. This happened in at least two cases, killing the drivers. A retired Brigadier of the REME, who had been in the Ministry of Supply when these vehicles were introduced into the British Army, told me that 'the Morris 1 ton truck had performed well in its trials on sand – on Margate beach'.

Authority was given for a Sharjah *dhow* to be chartered to supply the posts at Maghaira and Nakhla. This monthly delivery brought vehicle fuel and lubricants, dry rations (rice, maize flour, tinned food etc) as well as the fresh rations, such as onions and live goats, to both locations, plus Sharjah water in barrels for the post at Nakhla. As the consignments were not accompanied by a TOL representative, it usually happened that 'bad weather would force the *dhow* to put into Abu Dhabi for shelter'. The large goats loaded in Sharjah would find their way ashore in Abu Dhabi and be replaced by weak animals that only just survived the rest of the journey to Maghaira. In practice, only those troops in the squadron base ate the meat, usually about twice in the month.[6]

The loaded *dhow* came to the landing place at the time of high tide and grounded. First the drums of petrol were rolled over the side and floated ashore by the unloading party, swimming, and then pushed up timbers into the trucks which came as close to the water's edge as the terrain allowed. The drums had been used many times before so that sea water usually got into the contents. The lightened *dhow* then came closer inshore and, as the tide ebbed, the fatigue party could wade out and carry the stores on their backs to dry land. The goats swam ashore if they were fit enough. Finally, empty fuel drums were taken out to the *dhow* which floated off as the tide rose again.

From Maghaira, the *dhow* sailed westwards to an inlet to the east of Ras Khumais to unload the supplies for the Nakhla Post. Their water started off slightly brackish from the Sharjah supply and it too was carried in old 44-gallon drums that leaked adding to the salt content. Even so, this water was more potable than the water from the local wells on the Mijann, which were heavily contaminated with magnesium sulphate.[7]

During this month there was a visit by a team from GHQ Middle East Land Forces and Middle East Air Force to arrange the administrative transfer of the TOL to the Army.

Authority was given for some 112 recruits for the TOL from Aden to be flown in on the aircraft being sent to take the HQ and one squadron of the APL back home.

Eleven APL vehicles were left in Sharjah and sold to the TOL. One of these vehicles, a Bedford QL 3 tonner was in use until 1957 and must have dated from before 1945. In the course of time, the desert paint wore off in places showing the RAF blue underneath. Beneath many coats of this blue paint could be detected the outline of the divisional sign of the Wessex Division, indicating an earlier Army use, probably in north-west Europe after the D-Day landings.[8] 'Old Blue' as it became known, was driven for its last years by Corporal Driver Ali Nasr Habashi (Ali Shaiba) as no other driver could handle its idiosyncrasies or even start it.

September

Dress

The individual Arab soldier's clothing issue was based on the British tropical scale and consisted of:

Khaki Drill (KD) shirt and trousers
Olive drab denim fatigue trousers and blouse
White cotton cellular underwear (singlet and drawers)
Red *shmagh* with black *'agal* with single *khanjar* badge
Brown leather 'Sandals, Muscat Levies'
Dark blue cotton PT shorts
Black canvas PT shoes
Khaki jersey wool pullover
British Army greatcoat for winter wear
1938 pattern web belt and accoutrements including mess tins and an enamel drinking mug and knife, fork, and spoon

For most of the local recruits this wealth of possessions and clothing posed many problems as they may never have even seen pictures of many of these garments let alone know how they were worn, in particular the underwear.

Off duty, trousers and underpants were immediately taken off and replaced as soon as possible by the man's own *wazra* (loincloth) for greater coolness and comfort. Putting their trousers back on again they would often be donned over the *wazra*. Two yards of cotton loincloth do not rest naturally inside most pairs of trousers particularly if the occupant is marching or performing other military activities. Either the loincloth bunches up below the belt to give the wearer strange additional buttock or belly bulges, or it slips slowly down one trouser leg to emerge as a brightly coloured banner at ankle level.

Even after many months there were occasions when a drill parade would be interrupted for '*wazra* trouble in the ranks'. One *bedu* recruit is alleged to have managed to appear on parade with his trousers on back-to-front.

The 'Sandal, Muscat Levies' is of a particularly heavy pattern with one buckled strap to hold it in place. The origin of the design dated from the Muscat Levies raised during the Second World War but the provisional British War Office specification was not published until 18 August 1960. It had a stiff thick leather sole with a heel block complete with heel iron and a stiff heel cup carrying the brass buckle and the holding strap. The wide toe vang strap curled up and back to slot through the cross strap and end in a loop through which went the fastening strap (see Plate 31).

Once worn-in and properly fastened, they were very suitable footwear, letting sand in and out easily and protecting the foot on stony ground. There was, however, difficulty with the sandals when new and worn by recruits who had not realised how firmly they needed to be strapped on. The energetic stamping of feet during drill parades frequently resulted in a shower of discarded sandals falling to the ground, particularly at the 'About Turn' movement on the march. As most of the local recruits had gone barefoot all their lives, when not wearing light heelless sandals, these sandals were perhaps their greatest trial.

October

The reinforcement plan for the Gulf proposed by the British Middle East Office to the Foreign Office was that 250 RAF Regiment troops from the RAF base at Habbaniya in Iraq would be flown to the seat of the trouble equipped to light scales. After the transfer of responsibility for internal security in the Gulf, from the RAF to the British Army, it was planned that an infantry battalion, about 400 all ranks, again on light scales, would be flown in when required from within the Middle East Command.

Abdullah bin Salim al Ka'abi moved his base to Mahadha from Liwaif and Sharm.

In Buraimi, a camel caravan with rice for the Saudis was intercepted.

An Anson landed on the airstrip in the eastern Liwa at the Al Khis Post. The airstrip had been laid out by the TOL Arab officer from the Humar Post.

November

One of Turki's slaves defected to the TOL and applied for manumission, which was granted by the Political Agent. The freeing, or manumission, by the British authorities of those slaves who presented themselves had been carried out in the Trucial States since the early 1900s. This incident would have made a propaganda point showing the more liberal conditions in the Trucial States.

On 6 November, an Operational Directive was issued to the Commandant TOL by the Senior Army Officer Persian Gulf that he was

> to prevent arms, ammunition, supplies and re-inforcements from entering the territory of the Trucial States and to blockade the Saudis in Hamasa.

On 7 November, at about 1530 hours, Major Thwaites, RSM Daud Sidqi and Flying Officer A L C Duncan RAF Medical Officer were shot dead and Sergeant Chinn and Corporal Cruickshank were shot and wounded by three Adeni soldiers of C Squadron, who were manning Post 5 in the open area between the palm gardens of Buraimi and Sa'ara villages. The three Adenis fled into Hamasa village and sought sanctuary with the Saudis.

Sergeant Chinn, though himself wounded, was able to drive the seriously hurt Corporal Cruickshank back to the Squadron HQ and send a radio message to RHQ in Sharjah. The Arab officer of the squadron took over command.

Being a Saturday, the Commandant had gone for a picnic with his family but was found by the Duty Officer, Captain Steggles, and both officers drove down to Buraimi that night. The bodies of the dead were flown back to Sharjah the next day, escorted by Captain Steggles.

A Squadron under Major MacDonald followed and, on arrival, disarmed all Adeni soldiers and re-established the blockade of Hamasa. C Squadron had ceased to be effective.

Negotiations by Shaikh Zayed bin Sultan through Shaikh Saqr of Buraimi resulted in the arrest of the three murderers by Shaikh Zayed's men and their return to Sharjah for trial in Muscat as the killings took place in Sultanate territory.

Number 2 Squadron of the RAF Regiment were flown quickly to Sharjah from Habbaniya in accordance with the re-inforcement plan.

Some 90 of the Adeni troops in the force were discharged after screening and sent back to Aden. Those Adenis who remained continued to give loyal service to the end of their contracts.

The report dated 19 November on the inquiry into the tragedy stated that 'the Levies had been put into an operational role at much too early a stage in their training and that their training and administration had been gravely handicapped by wrangling over budgetary responsibility and their establishment resulting in lack of transport, personnel and stores'.

What the report did not comment upon was the unwise decision to recruit 'ex-APL personnel' for the TOL without ensuring adequate screening to discover why they had left the APL. This meant that a number of unreliable characters came to Sharjah to serve as mercenaries in a land where they owed neither loyalty nor allegiance and were only there for gain. The selling of their ammunition by a number of these men in Buraimi whilst reporting that it had been fired in action was the main reason for Major Thwaites and his party going to arrest the suspects. Post 5 was, of course, designed to provide fire positions covering its approaches and was a defensive position.

The report continued that the RAF Regiment squadron, which had been flown from Habbaniya to Sharjah immediately after the incident, would provide the firm military base and allow for good training programmes to be planned by the TOL and for their squadrons to be rotated. It concluded with the recommendation that 'the strain on the British staff [of the TOL] was too great and that a small increase in the establishment of a further two British officers was required'.

Recruitment of 60 local men, their personal serial numbers from 655 to 715 inclusive, who were all embodied together on 18 November, had been mainly through their Shaikhs. Among them were 656 Ali Batti Eisa, then a boy soldier, 669 Khamis Harib, 679 Khilfan Matr al Rumaithi, 681 Bakhit Musallim al Amiri and 715 Salim Awadh Yafai.

This had built up sufficient numbers for the creation of a local squadron which was under training in Sharjah and included a few local junior NCOs. The other NCOs and the SSM were Adenese of proven loyalty.

Those local men enlisted earlier, among them 642 Obaid Ali Rashid, who had enlisted a month or so before, had mostly been kept together in their own small sub-units and deployed, where possible under their own local NCOs such as Lance Corporal Khilfan

Matr Neyadi, to the various small outposts and in some of the posts blockading Hamasa.

December

In Buraimi there were a number of attempts by individuals to run the blockade only one of which was successfully achieved under covering fire from Hamasa village.

At the end of the year the force was deployed as follows:

Commandant	Lieutenant-Colonel Martin
RSM	WO Mohammed Ahmed
Chief Clerk	ORQMS Zaki Shwaihat
Clerks	Mr Nyer, Mr Menon
OC HQ Squadron	Captain Shaw
Paymaster	Sergeant Wilcox
Quartermaster	Captain Rowcliffe
RQMS	Staff Sergeant Thoma Attulla
MTO	Captain Steggles
MT Sergeant	Artificer Sergeant Playfor
Signals Sergeant	Sergeant Said Mahsin
A Squadron	Mulazim Hydra Shaikh
re-formed and under training in Sharjah	
B Squadron (Tarif)	Captain Warner, Adeni Mulazim
HQ Maghaira outposts at Agaila, Nakhla	
C Squadron (Buraimi)	Major MacDonald, Adeni Mulazim
HQ Murab'a Zayed with outposts at Jimi, Ghafat Shahine, Sa'ara, Qatara and, additionally, in Qasr al Khadaq Buraimi (under command Corporal Mohammed Nakhaira)	
D Squadron (Sharjah)	Captain Criddle (on sick leave)
in reserve with outposts at Wadi Qaur, Burj Obaid	
Liwa Posts	Mulazim Abdulla Hussain
Humar and Al Khis	

World Events 1953

January	Yugoslavia	Josip Tito elected President.
March	Moscow	Joseph Stalin died.
March	New York	Swedish Dag Hammarskjöld chosen to succeed Trygve Lie as Secretary-General of the United Nations.
May	Baghdad	King Faisal II of Iraq crowned. Nuri Said was the Prime Minister.
June	Nepal	Mount Everest conquered.
June	London	Queen Elizabeth II crowned.
July	Pyongyang	Korean War ends.
August	Iran	Military coup overthrows Mohammed Mossadegh and restores Shah to power.
November	Riyadh	King Abdul Aziz ibn Abdul Rahman al Saud died and was succeeded by his son Crown Prince Saud.

Notes

1 The RAF Regiment are the ground troops of the RAF responsible for their local anti-aircraft and ground defence. Organised in squadrons and flights equivalent to infantry companies and platoons, they were equipped with light armoured cars, Landrovers and 40mm Bofors guns. In Iraq and Aden, the RAF Regiment provided the British element of the Levies there.

2 Bait Turki was built for Turki bin Ataishan on the south-west corner of the Hamasa village overlooking the *wadi*. Turki's headquarters were within the walled enclosure which had a small gatehouse on the western wall. There was an upper room opening onto a walled patio on the flat roof of the rooms below.

3 Bait Aqeel was built for Turki's assistant of that name at the north end of the village in open ground.

4 The Bani Ka'ab tribe nominally owed allegiance to the Sultan of Muscat but, like others, had received little or no material support from him for many years. Being poor they were ripe for subversion and were now divided into a pro-Saudi, faction under Obaid bin Juma based in Khatwa, and an anti-Saudi group, under Abdullah bin Salim of Mahadha, who placed their allegiance with the nearest influential leader in the absence of the Sultan of Muscat, in this case Shaikh Zayed.

5 There is a picture captioned 'TOL tents – Markhia, May 1953', in Ron Codrai's book on Abu Dhabi, *The Seven Shaikhdoms*, published by Stacey International 1990, indicating that there were probably additional small posts with PDTC field-party camps.

6 The system was later changed and a meat allowance was paid to the troops in these outstations.

7 Epsom Salts, known locally as *melkh inglizi*.
8 The letter W on a bar.

6

1954

January

Major E F Johnson MBE MC, South Lancashire Regiment, and myself, both joined the TOL on 6 January 1954.

Major Johnson filled the vacant post of second-in-command.

I came direct from the Middle East Centre for Arabic Studies in the Lebanon as a lieutenant in the Queens Royal Regiment, was appointed Local Acting Captain (unpaid) and assigned to command A Squadron, which was under training in Sharjah.[1]

Also in January, Lieutenant P S Allfree, East Surrey Regiment, joined from the Suez Canal Zone and was appointed Local Acting Captain as Adjutant for a short time and then given responsibilities for recruit training in Sharjah.

A working party of Mulazim Hydra Shaikh (ex-APL), Quartermaster Sergeant Toma Attullah (Arab Legion) and myself was formed to study the British Army Drill Book and devise suitable Arabic words of command. At the end of the month, Mulazim Hydra commanded a Guard of Honour from A Squadron for the new Commander-in-Chief Middle East, who was visiting the unit at which Arabic words of command were used for the first time in public.[2]

The rifle range used by the TOL near Sharjah was in the dunes to the east, beside the track to one of the water wells used by the people of Sharjah and within marching distance of camp. One minor disadvantage was that firing had to stop whenever a man on his donkey came past, or right through, the range itself. The range backstop bullet catcher was a dune slightly larger than the others in the area and the red safety flags carefully put up around the notional danger area meant nothing to the local inhabitants, except that they indicated a possible reference to the 'national' flags of the Sultan of Muscat and the Ruler of Abu Dhabi.[3] The range was basic, without any installations for butts or target mechanisms. The four-foot square targets in their wooden frames were stuck in the sand in front of this special dune and the firing point paced out at the chosen distance on the convenient stretch of flat ground.

With the expectation that recruits who had carried firearms since puberty would be good shots, very few were found to be so. It was reported that nine out of ten shots on the whole four-foot square target at 200 yards range would be the occasion for congratulations. The actual scoring of 'bulls and inners' came later.

Despite the lack of training aids, the need to improvise and the total illiteracy of the recruits, no instructor ever had cause at that time to complain of lack of keeness and enthusiasm on the part of the soldiers in their six weeks' basic training. At first, because few if any, of the *bedu* had any idea what a drill parade was or looked like, before the days of television or even newspapers, new recruits would applaud their instructor's demonstration of an arms drill movement and discussions would break out in the ranks over their own performance. Unlike any other force under British Army tutelage, the TOL was unique in that there was no comparable local military tradition to build on and everything had to be taught, and learnt, from the absolute beginning.

The unit badge was also unique, being a single but sheathed right-handed *khanjar*. Naked blades of the various forms of ethnic daggers, swords, and spears are used in the emblems of other regiments and military forces worldwide. Unusual too was that the officers wore a different badge, right-handed and left-handed *khanjars* crossed (I am still looking for a real left-handed *khanjar*).

February

My A Squadron was the first to be recruited locally and I allocated the men to their troops and sections to ensure an even mixture of tribes and origins throughout the squadron. No sub-unit or section was made up of men from one tribe or clan. My aim was to discourage the settlement of their tribal fueds whilst serving and to substitute our squadron as their military tribe.

The squadron establishment was of an HQ and three troops each commanded by a sergeant with three sections of ten rank and file. Each troop travelled in three Morris trucks. The squadron commander had one Landrover and the squadron second-in-command, the squadron sergeant major and the squadron quartermaster sergeant, with the cook and storeman, travelled in the two Bedfords and the Morris water cart that made up the HQ group. Excluding drivers, radio operators, fitters and the medical orderly attached from HQ Squadron, the strength was about 100 all ranks.

The squadron in the western area had the tasks of covering the routes into the Trucial States from the west, to detect, report and oppose any further incursion from Saudi Arabia and to provide local protection for PDTC drilling and exploration operations.

On 8 February, A Squadron left Sharjah in a convoy of 13 vehicles at noon to relieve Captain Warner's B Squadron at Maghaira. The convoy was delayed by heavy rain between Jabal Ali and Muqattara and arrived at 0330 hours. The whole convoy was halted on the track through the Sih Shuwaib *sabkhat* in ankle-deep water when my Landrover's engine got wet. Until it dried out again no movement was possible as deep ruts in the *sabkhat* on both sides of the track were quite impassable. Later this stretch of *sabkhat* became known to the unit as *Moumin's Sabkhat* in honour of the driver of that name whose vehicle got stuck in one of these ruts for a fortnight. He, of course, remained with his vehicle until it was recovered to Sharjah, being supplied by passing TOL vehicles.

Local positions and the main outposts at Agaila and Nakhla were taken over during the next two days. B Squadron returned to Sharjah transferring Mulazim Abdullah Hussain to A Squadron.

A Squadron was deployed with one troop split between Agaila Post 3 in the Bainuna and the location known as Nakhla Post 5 on the track across the Mijann plateau.

At Agaila, near the well of that name, there was one section with its Morris truck, one No 19 radio set and signaller under command of the Sergeant Troop Commander.

At Nakhla, there were the other two sections with their two Morris trucks, one No 19 radio set and signaller under command of an additional Arab officer, Mulazim Abdullah Hussain, responsible for patrolling the Mijann plateau and guarding the main route from the west (see Plate 7).

The second troop was deployed in and around the squadron base at Maghaira, to the west of Tarif, with one section split between a watchpost near the drilling rig at Murban and a watch post on the top of a hill feature some distance south of Maghaira. One section guarded the squadron base leaving the third section available for duties around the camp but at five minutes' notice with their Morris truck for rapid response in the local area (see Plate 5).

ABOVE LEFT. **Clayton Force patrol, Mijann, November 1955.** On the lip of the large dune overlooking Uglat Nakhla. On this patrol, my Landrover with sand tyres, had a front-mounted Bren gun, the other two had Bren guns on tailgate mounts and road tyres (see Plate 16). ABOVE RIGHT. **Live firing exercise by RAF Venoms, Mijann, December 1955.** Air-strike support demonstration for Clayton Force at the old Post 5 Nakhla site using 20mm cannon to attack oil-drum targets (see Plate 16). BELOW. **Recruits passing-out parade, Sharjah, March 1956.** Lieutenant-Colonel Johnson, RSM Richardson, Squad Sergeant, Captain Adams and RSM Mohammed Ahmed, after inspecting the squad. The parade ground was bare-rolled dry *sabkhat*.

ABOVE. **The Officers of the Trucial Oman Levies, Sharjah, February 1954.** *Standing left to right*: Adeni Mulazim; Adeni Mulazim; Captain Rowcliffe, QM; Captain Shaw, HQ Squadron; Captain Steggles, MTO; Adeni Mulazim; Mulazim Hydra Shaikh, A Squadron *seated left to right*: Captain Warner, B Squadron; Major MacDonald, D Squadron; Captain Allfree, Adjutant; Lieutenant-Colonel Martin, CO; Major Johnson, 2i/c; Captain Criddle, C Squadron; Captain Clayton, A Squadron.
BELOW. **The watchpost at Murban, Tarif, March 1954**. The huts housed one section here being visited by Mulazim Hydra Shaikh 2i/c. A Squadron. The paint was stripped from the front of my Landrover driving into sandstorms.

ABOVE LEFT. **Post 4 Buraimi on the track to Hafit near Al Ain, August 1954.** The quickly built signal hut with salvaged tentage over the usual flat roof. Jabal Hafit is in the distance. The white stones mark the camp perimeter, a small parade ground in front of the line of huts with the administrative area behind. ABOVE RIGHT. **Post 5 Nakhla on the track across the Mijann, March 1954.** The two Morris 1-ton trucks are by the signal hut, which the Mulazim shared with the signaller. The tents housed the two sections manning the Post. The owner of the camels had come from Saudi Arabia and had been detained for questioning. BELOW. **Avro Anson MkXIX of 1417 Comns Flight RAF, Tarif, May 1954.** There was a small RAF maintenance crew stationed in their own camp on the Tarif hill east of the PDTC base location. The airstrip was on the *sabkhat* to the south-west.

ABOVE. **IO's patrol to Masafi, April 1956**. In the lower part of Wadi Siggi on the way up to Masafi from the south. This was the easy but our homeward route from Masafi came down the Wadi 'Asima. BELOW LEFT. **Murabba' Zayed, Al Ain, February 1957.** During the blockade of Hamasa the tower was the centre of a *barusti* camp housing the TOL squadron base. The date gardens of Buraimi and Sa'ara are to the left in the distance. BELOW RIGHT. **Jahili Tower, Al Ain, June 1956.** The Jahili Fort became the TOL squadron base in November 1955. The tower was the look-out post and the duty men used the *barusti* shelter just visible under the doorway with the rope to climb up. The troops lived in the main keep of the fort and the officers and squadron HQ in the courtyard west of the main entrance. The big tower had been in this condition for years.

ABOVE. **Jahili Fort, Al Ain, June 1956, midday.** The main entrance arch had been rebuilt, the squadron signboard erected and the flagpole raised. The radio masts are on the corner tower of the main fort and against the far courtyard wall in the administrative area. BELOW. **Jahili Fort, Al Ain, June 1956, sunset.** Looking from the tower Eastwards across the main courtyard vehicle park towards Al Ain date gardens with the tabletop of Jabal Qatar in the distance. The Morris water truck, Bedford QL and some of the squadron Landrovers are in the foreground.

ABOVE. **The new squadron base at Kahil, Mahadha, August 1954.** Outside the Buraimi Neutral Zone to where the TOL had withdrawn. The officer's *barusti* is in the centre with his bed outside under a shade. A very dusty place among the thorn trees within the foothills. BELOW. **Post 4 Buraimi, December 1955.** My hut and front garden. The whole camp had been rebuilt with pitched roofs covered with palm matting over the *barusti* rafters.

ABOVE LEFT. **Clayton Force, Mijann, December 1955.** Myself as callsign '2AL17', Transmitting a practice airstrike request from my Landrover. The 2 inch mortar and signal pistol are ready for target indication. ABOVE RIGHT. **Post 4 Buraimi, January 1955.** The signboard was home-made to show the military nature of the post. The cat was the daughter of Aziza who had 'looked after' the squadron at Murabba' Zayed before they moved to Kahil but would not go with them or transfer to the new Post 4. The pyramid tent was my shelter during the rains. BELOW. **C Squadron vehicles from Tarif, July 1955.** Bedford RL and early Landrover newly arrived, with retread 700 X 16 road tyres, at the headland west of Mirfa to unload supply *dhow*.

ABOVE. **IO's Liwa patrol, Habshan, December 1956.** Adjusting pressures on the newly arrived sand tyres on new Landrovers before entering the sands; Staff Sergeant Emil Gosous behind the door of the far vehicle; Corporal Salim Awadh crouching at the front of the centre one and Major Bridges standing by my vehicle on the right. BELOW LEFT. **IO's Liwa patrol, Qufa, January 1957**. Halted on the hard sand near the top of a dune at midday. The third vehicle is hidden by the nearest one. Square canvas water bags had become a standard issue and hung on the Landrovers. BELOW RIGHT. **Political Resident's Escort to Abu Dhabi, March 1957.** Halted on the track on the Mahawi feature before going down onto the *Sabkhat* leading to the Maqta' and the Abu Dhabi causeway.

The remaining troop were available for training under their troop commander and the squadron second-in-command, Mulazim Hydra Shaikh, and as the squadron reserve.

Squadron headquarters was at Maghaira where Squadron Sergeant Major Salim Shaikh, the SQMS, storeman and stores, medical orderly, fitter Sergeant Emil Gosous, the cook, No 19 radio set and signaller were located together with remainder of the squadron vehicles.

The two small detachments in the Liwa reported by radio to Post 4 at Maghaira but were under direct command of Sharjah HQ.

An Anson aircraft of 1417 Communication Flight RAF operated from the Tarif airstrip for five days in the week. Its task was to carry out daily patrols of the Liwa and the western areas of the territory out to the Saudi frontier in support of the TOL on the ground. The HF radio set in the Anson could be tuned to the TOL frequency and work to their No 19 sets (see Plate 8).

On Fridays, I used to fly in the Anson over the Al Khis and Humar Posts in the Liwa and speak to the radio operators there by radio as no landings were allowed except in special circumstances. Sometimes there was mail to be dropped and the NCOs in charge of the posts 'turned out the guard' to salute the aircraft as it flew by at low level. The co-operation between the Anson crews and the TOL was very close and made a significant contribution not only to the control of the western area but also to all the TOL's operations.

A Squadron training programmes were limited to weapon training, drill, physical training and deployment practice. Ammunition shortages meant that live firing was restricted to basic range work so that the soldiers pay classification could be determined by their skill-at-arms on rifle and Bren gun. No sub-machine guns were issued and neither were grenades. The only two-inch mortar ammunition available was for operational use only. The terrain, temperature and the squadron's operational role and tasks there meant that battle tactics training, apart from basic fire control, was pointless.

As summer approached, the daily routine became more and more that of keeping clean weapons and equipment and repairing the ragged tentage and other shelters in which the men lived. Rotation of the troops around the various posts and duties within the squadron was at three-week intervals for the outstations and weekly at the local watchposts. These watchposts and the larger outposts had a sentry always on look-out duty by day and night. This reduced the men's daily routine to regular spells of duty, sleeping and camp fatigues and cooking in living conditions not much better than the poorest *bedu*.

At the Nakhla Post there were two Morris trucks so the *mulazim* in command there could carry out motor patrols over the areas of good 'going' on the Mijann plateau during which *dhubb* lizards were hunted to supplement the rations. Mulazim Abdullah Hussain, late of the APL Camel Patrol was in his element in the outpost. I made the mistake of swopping over my two *mulazims* for a change of duties. After only a few days our squadron base at Maghaira had ceased to run smoothly under Mulazim Abdullah and Mulazim Hydra, away at Nakhla, was sending plaintive messages asking where to go on patrol. Within a week both *mulazims* were back where they belonged.

The Muscat Field Force, with the Petroleum Development Oman oil-company party, landed over the beach at Duqm on the Omani coast opposite Masirah Island and established a base there.

A TOL detachment was sent to Mahadha temporarily.

The British Agency that had been in Sharjah since 1823 was closed on 24 February. It was re-opened in the new buildings on the Dubai creekside on 1 March.

The old Agency building in Sharjah became the TOL British Officers' Mess as there was now a need for it to be separate from the RAF Officers' Mess. The possible risks of having the British officers living so far away from their troops were not considered at that time to be relevant. There was a generator for electricity, electric lights and a few rooms were fitted with air-conditioning units, however it was laid out for one or two Europeans with a large household staff. It was some time before the facilities were suitable for about ten British officers with a small mess staff. The sanitary arrangements never did reach the standard required.

Colonel Martin lived with his family in a rented house on the creekside on the southern edge of Sharjah town. This building had a first-floor toilet facility directly over the water.

The multi-place bucket latrine installation in the Levies Camp was the only such facility in the unit. Outstations, large and small, were sufficiently far from other habitation for areas of desert to be designated as 'Latrine Areas'. The hot sun, dung beetles and other natural forces were usually sufficient for safe disposal. At Maghaira, the troops' area was in the broken ground south of the camp. The officer's hut, being on the seaward side, had no natural cover so a single bucket 'Thunder box', suitably screened, had been built. In Buraimi at Murabba' Zayed, the troops did have a long walk to the designated areas and the officer went afar by Landrover, the front bumper of which is a functional seat.

March

There was a severe sandstorm in the Tarif area which blew down most of the A Squadron camp so, for many days, the reserve troop became fully employed rebuilding the camp. The huts in this camp were constructed from *chandal* poles and palm matting tied together with coconut-fibre lashings. The squadron's outstations also used a 180-pounder tent as the radio shack. The tents were faded and torn but replacements were not available. The local watchposts were made from sand-filled oil drums and old tentage and palm matting.

At night, over the whole of the Trucial States, the total absence of artificial light meant that any vehicle using headlamps could be seen for great distances by the glow on the horizon. The headlamps of trucks heading west over the high ground at Ruwais could be seen from Agaila. The glow from the Qatar oil company at Umm Said was visible from the Nakhla Post and the red light on the top of the radio mast in Sharjah could be seen from the track over the rise of Jabal Ali. This was a welcome sight to the tired driver who had driven from Tarif or Maghaira through the night to escape the heat of the day, as it meant that he could rest until dawn then drive the last fifty kilometres into Sharjah in time for breakfast.

Radio communication was only between the static posts using Second World War No 19 radio sets, low power, most of which had been made in Canada and had markings in Russian. The Arab (originally Adeni) operators used English Morse with a mixture of Army and civil procedures (Z and Q codes) on CW (carrier wave) with surprisingly good results under frequently bad conditions. Voice communication was normally restricted to officer-to-officer conversations after contact had been made by Morse. Each post had its fixed schedules for calling HQ Sharjah on the command-net frequency. Other frequencies were used for post-to-post conversations between the Arab operators which often went like this:

''Allo, two alpha lima three, this is two alpha lima four – 'ow do you 'ear me? Over.'

''Allo, two alpha lima four, hinna two alpha lima three – 'ear you stringeth five – ya Mohammed kayf khalek? – over.'

Despite their mixture of procedures and language the early radio operators of the TOL established a tradition of a very high standard of operating in their speed and accuracy of Morse and net discipline and also their care for and tuning of their sets. It was 'idle and unprofessional' to use the MCW (modulated carrier wave) mode for Morse transmissions, which the sender could also hear in his headphones and covered a wider bandwidth, instead of CW, for which both sets had to be exactly on the same frequency to exclude interference. Of course, each operator could instantly recognise his colleagues' 'fist', or sending characteristics, which led to a stranger not getting responses to his calls on the net, as happened to me when I first came on the air using Morse as 2AL17.

The unit call sign 'Two Alpha Lima' was never changed from its adoption very early on and was still in use at the end of 1960. Signal security was minimal in the normal military radio procedure sense, except for the use of nicknames for local personalities and tribes, again unchanged and often compromised in the context of the transmission.

B Squadron, under Captain Warner, was now established at the Post at Wadi Qaur, with an outpost at Burj Obaid, having relieved D Squadron, which was very under-strength.

In Buraimi, Shaikh Saqr al Na'imi was failing to enforce the blockade of Hamasa in the sector under his responsibility. This was having a harmful effect on the morale of the C Squadron posts in the other sectors and reducing the effect of the blockade.

In Dubai, the shaikhs invited the officers of the TOL to an *azima* that marked the beginning of a new relationship.[4] The preoccupation of the TOL with Buraimi and the problems of the Shaikhs of Abu Dhabi had perhaps prevented the TOL from making close contacts with the Shaikhs of Dubai and this event was a public signal of friendship and co-operation.

On 20 March, a TOL patrol from Sharjah accompanied the Agency Arab Assistant (Mr Ali Bustani) to Masafi to investigate the building of a wall across the road between the two villages by the Fujairah people and their building of two 'towers' overlooking the Ras al Khaima village. Trouble was averted and the Ruler of Fujairah invited to visit the British Agency in Dubai to resolve the matter.

Local recruitment had continued, including 785 Ismail Saddiq Othman. Most recruits were destined for D Squadron, which was in reserve and under training in Sharjah. The Basic Training Team instructors included Sergeant Salimeen Salem.

April

In Buraimi it was reported that Shaikh Saqr was receiving large sums of money as a result of his breaches in the blockade of Hamasa.

At about this time Corporal Driver Ali Nasr Habashi arrived at Maghaira with load of petrol in drums for A Squadron in his 3-tonner 'Old Blue'. There was mud all down one side of the truck but no other damage. Twenty-five drums were unloaded and Corporal Ali prepared to depart with a load of empty drums on his 250-kilometre journey back to Sharjah when someone asked him about the mud. He replied, 'Yes, we slipped off the track into the *sabkhat*. Had to unload and a passing oil-company truck helped us back onto the road and to re-load.' He always travelled alone so the 'we' and 'us' refers to himself and the lorry. One of the first local drivers to be enlisted into the TOL, he helped to establish the tradition among the Transport Section drivers of self-sufficiency and determination to reach their destination with their cargo under all circumstances. When not required for driving, Corporal Ali Nasr was a vehicle maintenance instructor for new drivers. The principal driving instructors were Sergeant Mohammed Saleh, Corporal Yousef Eid and Lance Corporal Said Salim Si'ar.

Funding of £1,350 was agreed for the building of a prison within the TOL compound to hold TOL and civilians under British jurisdiction. The care of such civilian prisoners was added to the TOL's responsibilities.

May

On 2 May the Imam died in Nizwa and was succeeded by Ghalib bin Ali al Hinawi.[5]

Life for the British officers in the outstations took a turn for the better when kerosene refrigerators were issued. As it was an administrative impossibility to provide one European monthly ration for each British officer in the outstations from the RAF stores in Sharjah, a 'ration allowance' of seven shillings and sixpence per day was paid. The problem then passed to the officer – where to spend it in the middle of a desert and what to buy? The obvious answer 'the sandwiches there' did not help. Until then, their meals had consisted of a whole tin of 'whatever' as there was no means of keeping any uneaten food. The choice of tins of 'whatever' was limited by what could be bought in Dubai *suq* from Lalchand's small shop. Sardines, lambs' tongues in aspic, condensed Scotch broth, Russian salad, Jacobs Cream Crackers, tinned cheese and tinned mandarin oranges were the total menu available. Military staples such as 'bully beef', 'M + V', baked beans were not to be found, even a loaf of bread was unobtainable. Where there was a PDTC camp nearby, such as at Tarif, the British officer was made welcome, not only for the occassional shower in fresh water but also to share their meals. Without this kindness, the health of many TOL and TOS officers would have suffered.

In Muscat, the three Adenis accused of murdering Major Thwaites, RSM Daud and the RAF doctor were tried by the Sharia Court. The evidence was said to be insufficient for murder under Sharia law so the three were to remain in prison *sine die*, or indefinitely.

In Buraimi, Turki put out a post south-west of Hamasa itself which in turn brought about the relocation of two TOL posts in the area and the establishment of one further TOL post.

Two British NCOs from the TOL Workshops in Sharjah drove into Hamasa in the dark having lost their way. They were detained for two days as guests by Turki bin Ataishan.

In Sharjah, 2 Squadron RAF Regiment had been replaced by another which started energetic midday fitness parades and had some heat-stroke casualties. To prove their desert-worthiness, they sent a Landrover patrol to Buraimi, but did not tell the TOL. Some hours later one RAF Landrover returned to report that the others had got lost. Fortunately, the TOL quickly found a number of individuals sitting under thorn trees with empty water bottles and their Landrovers stuck in the sand just beyond Ud al Matina. Later, to make up for this débâcle, the Squadron proposed to travel to the west along the coastal track to 'reconnoitre the Saudi border' but were advised that, as beyond Mirfa the track was not clearly marked, the TOL squadron (mine) in the area would detain them by force if necessary.

The administration of the TOL now started to come under the British Army system. With all its additional paperwork it was perhaps unsuited to an active service unit where only the few British ranks could write. In particular, documentation for vehicle use had to be implemented, 'work tickets' filled in, permits to drive issued etc.

These formalities were perhaps workable in the Sharjah base area but were ignored by the lone British officer in the outstations.

Towards the end of May, an ARAMCO exploration party with an armed Saudi escort started work in the 'Udaid Peninsula. An Anson dropped a message to the ARAMCO party to demand their withdrawal which was ignored. To counter this incursion, a TOL force under Major Johnson made up of the reserve troop from A Squadron from Maghaira and two troops from Sharjah, with Captains Steggles and Allfree and Sergeant Playfor with Landrovers and Morris trucks, were sent to land on the eastern shore of the 'Udaid Peninsula. They were to be supported by HMS *Flamingo* and transported in a landing craft.

I went up to the Nakhla Post on 25 May and Captain Shaw moved to Maghaira with a Royal Navy signaller to maintain communication with the ships. The beach landing was successful but had perhaps been given sufficient publicity to enable the ARAMCO party to withdraw to Saudi Arabia in good time. I had reported from Nakhla on 26 May my interception of radio conversations between the Americans in the ARAMCO party and their families in Dhahran clearly giving the date of their return home. Nevertheless, the operation proceeded as a show of force and much valuable training was gained.

In accordance with the new administrative regulations issued by the Command Secretary in Aden, all vehicles on this operation had to carry 'work tickets' authorising their movement.

June

On 17 June, Captain Shaw relieved me at Nakhla and linked up with the 'Udaid force a few days later. The composite force re-embarked and returned to Sharjah by the end of the month.

July

Staff Sergeant Hassan Abdulla Noman took over the Orderly Room duties of WO Zaki Shwaihat, who returned to Jordan.

In Buraimi, it was reported that the efficiency of the blockade had been improved. Shooting incidents had increased around Hamasa resulting in four blockade runners being killed, two captured and one camel killed during the month.

On 30 July in Jeddah, the Saudi Arabian and British Governments agreed to refer the 'Buraimi Dispute' to arbitration by an international tribunal. The main terms of this agreement were that the Saudi party under Turki bin Ataishan was to leave Hamasa and return to Saudi Arabia; the TOL squadron that had been surrounding it in Hamasa was to withdraw from the Buraimi Oasis; the country west and south of a line from Mirfa to Buraimi was territory under dispute; and that the TOL were to be reduced in strength by one squadron. A neutral zone of 15 miles radius, with its centre on Buraimi village, was to be policed by a joint force of 15 all ranks from the TOL with a similar number from Saudi Arabia and both sides were to refrain from any activity which would change the situation existing at that time.

As A Squadron had been away from base for six months and was by then very under strength and the men in need of re-kitting, it was decided that this was the squadron to be disbanded and the men sent to reinforce the permitted remaining three squadrons, less those selected for duty in Buraimi. D Squadron would thereupon be renamed A Squadron.

Captain Shaw took over command of B Squadron from Captain Warner who became Paymaster and OC HQ Squadron.

August

Captain Shaw with B Squadron relieved A Squadron at Maghaira at the beginning of August and had been briefed on the arrangements for meeting and escorting the replacement Saudi party towards Buraimi and escorting the departing party under Turki bin Ataishan out of the country. A Squadron returned to Sharjah on 3 August and most of it dispersed on leave, returning to new locations later.

By 8 August, Major MacDonald had withdrawn C Squadron to its new location at Kahil Post 1 (near Mahadha) outside the Buraimi Zone (see Plate 14). The blockade watchposts remained in place until the departure of Turki and his party.

The TOL detachment of 15 all ranks for the joint police force to be stationed in Buraimi drove to Kahil overnight on 8 August. They were: myself, Sergeant Ali Salem Nayadi, Corporal Harib Khilfan Nayadi, Lance Corporal Masoud Said Saman, and 9 specially selected men from A Squadron, including 679 Khilfan Matr al Rumaithi, 669 Khaimis Harib, Hilal Said Nayadi, Said Fahad Qitabi, 681 Bakhit Musallim al Amiri, Said Masoud al Qatabi, Hamoud Zaid Yafa'i (orderly), an Adeni driver and Signaller Mohammed Ahmed Adeni.

We had one Morris 1-ton truck and one Landrover, one WS No

19 radio station and were armed only with rifles, 50 rounds of ammunition each, and the officer's revolver with 12 rounds of ammunition.

On the morning of 9 August, the Saudi 'Police' party, under Major Abdullah bin Nami of the Saudi National Guard, was escorted into the area on the Haza al Baush route from the coast and was met by Major Johnson and myself in the Sulaimat area. As the TOL reception party had expected a uniformed military detachment from the Saudi Arabian National Guard, it had laid on a formal military reception which, nevertheless, did 'Present Arms' to the Saudi commander and his armed civilians.

Major Abdullah bin Nami had trained in Taif with the British Military Mission and knew its British officers. It was fortunate that I recognised the clerk to the Saudi party, Abdullah Quraishi, whom I had met under very different circumstances the previous year. It was perhaps equally fortunate that Quraishi did not recognise me.

It had been understood by the terms of the Agreement that both 'Police' units would move together to the site that I had selected well away from any villages and set up our camps without making contact with the outgoing parties. This was in the hope that there would be a clean break with the past and to prevent Turki bin Ataishan publically appearing to be handing over his 'Governorship' to the incoming Saudi representative. In the event, in contravention of the terms of the Agreement, Abdullah bin Nami and Abdullah Quraishi went directly to Turki in Hamasa.

In the afternoon that day, Major Johnson ordered me to go alone to enter Bait Turki on the south-west corner of Hamasa and demand of Turki bin Ataishan that he and his party evacuate the place immediately and proceed to Saudi Arabia. Being unsure of the nature of my reception upon attempting to enter the building, I approached in my Landrover along the *wadi* bed in a westerly direction through the *suq* area and arrived at the entrance without having been observed from afar. Though instructed to carry out this mission alone, I took with me Jundi 679 Khilfan Matr as escort and to remain in the Landrover.

The entrance door and its armed guard were on my right-hand side so I was able to get out of the driving seat on that side swiftly, say '*Salaam Alaykum*' to the startled guard before he could bring up his rifle, and enter the courtyard beyond. There I found Turki and Abdulla bin Nami sitting together, greeted them and, after the usual exchange of courtesies, relayed the demand. This demand I returned to repeat in less dramatic a fashion on each of the following three days, being accompanied by Major Johnson on the final occasion on 12 August.

Turki bin Ataishan and his party left Hamasa on the morning of 13 August 1954 after an occupation lasting nearly two years. They refused to be escorted out of the territory, lost their way, had many vehicle breakdowns and were scattered along the 80 miles between Mugattara and Maghaira. They were rescued by Major Johnson and Sergeant Mohammed Saleh and conducted out of the territory through Mirfa and Nakhla.

Two parts of the joint Buraimi Police camp were to the east of the track to Hafit about 1,000 yards from Falaj al Sarouj Al Ain. The TOL camp was some 200 yards west of the Saudi site and close to the track to Mazyad and Hafit about 1,000 yards south-east of the Falaj. It became known locally as 'Markaz al Sarouj' but to the TOL we were 2AL4 or Post 4.[6] (See Plates 6, 15, 17).

B Squadron then withdrew to be based on the PDTC camp at Tarif in the old RAF detachment huts with one section at Mirfa, two sections at Muqattara and one section on the Dab'iyyah peninsula. The Liwa Posts were also withdrawn back to Sharjah.

C Squadron, under Major MacDonald, was based at Kahil with one troop under a *mulazim* at Khatwa and another troop also commanded by a *mulazim* with posts in the Wadi Qaur.

There had been incidents of banditry in the Wadi Qaur to which the TOL responded by setting up the three posts in the area.

September

The September pay round was carried out by Captain Allfree as Captain Warner was on leave.

Captain Steggles took over command of C Squadron from Major MacDonald at Kahil in late September and Captain Huntingdon from Bahrain was attached to the Squadron.[7]

There were reports that Shaikh Obaid bin Juma of the Beni Ka'ab was collecting together about 150 tribesmen in the Wadi Jizzi area for operations against the Sultan of Muscat.

October

On 12 October, Ibri fell to the rebel Imam Ghalib bin Ali's forces under his brother, Talib, and on 16 October the Shaikhs of Ibri, loyal to the Sultan arrived at Qahil. These included Shaikhs Mohammed bin Abdullah al Yaqoobi, Ali bin Hilai al Duru'i and Hamed bin Saif al Kalbani.

At about this time, I called upon Shaikh Zayed at Al Muwaiqi to discuss the situation outside the Neutral Zone. After supper, our conversation turned to our thoughts and hopes for the future. Shaikh Zayed said that he wanted to see the day, with Allah's permission, that he would see the Oasis and the land green. Truly prophetic. I said that I hoped again to command a squadron of the TOL and to be stationed in the Oasis in the Jahili Fort, then derelict and being used to store locust poison. It was a classic example of Arab military architecture, which I said, and should be used for a more honourable purpose. This I did not achieve myself but others did.

A Dodge Power Wagon vehicle marked with the camel 'brand' of the Emir Abdulla bin Jaluwi, the governor of the Eastern Province of Saudi Arabia, arrived at 1900 hours after dark without having obtained prior clearance and having traversed disputed territory. It went directly to the Saudi camp. Shaikh Rashid bin Hamed, his brother and son all dined there with Bin Nami that night. The next day there was a report of a meeting in Hamasa of pro-Saudi Shaikhs to ally the Na'im from Hafit and the Bani Ka'ab in the Wadi Jizzi against the Sultan of Oman. On the 23 October, the Saudi Power-Wagon departed to the west.

The TOL Post at Khatwa overlooked the village where Obaid bin Juma al Ka'abi had been reported again as intending to return to take his part in the uprising.

On 25 October, the Wali from Sohar and some of his *askaris*, escorted by most of C Squadron under Captain Steggles, were moving into the area of Khatwa when a civilian refused to stop when challenged by the Wali's men. He was shot dead and was found to be carrying messages from Hamasa to Khatwa. C Squadron made a frontal attack on the village supported by Bani Ka'ab tribesmen loyal to Abdullah bin Salim. The action was successful and Obaid bin Juma's men dispersed to their villages. Levy 666 Khalais al Nayadi of Al Ain was killed in this action. Although this operation was not ordered by higher authority and took place on the initiative of the local commander, the action taken was later fully endorsed by the Political Agent.

Major Johnson arrived from Sharjah on 26 October to act as commander at Kahil whilst Captain Steggles and Mulazim Hydra consolidated positions in the Wadi Jizzi area. Sergeant Mohammed Nakhaira had remained at the Squadron's base in Kahil.

Also on 25 October, the Muscat and Oman Field Force started from Fahud, recapturing Ibri on 27 October.[8] This operation was undertaken by the officers in the field without the sanction of the Sultan but, with the co-incident action in the Wadi Jizzi, was to have far-reaching effects on the future of both the Sultanate of Oman and the Shaikhdom of Abu Dhabi.

On 31 October, Lieut-Col Martin visited Kahil with the newly arrived second-in command designate Major N C Smith, Essex Regiment, who also had previously served with him in the British Military Mission in Taif.

November

In early November, the hand-over of command of the TOL by Lieut-Col Martin to Major Johnson was completed. Major Johnson was promoted to Lieutenant-Colonel.

The C Squadron posts at Khatwa and the entrance to Wadi Qaur were withdrawn. The posts at Howailat at the eastern end of the Wadi Qaur and Sba'at in the Wadi Jizzi remained in position. Most of the squadron then set to work to build the road behind the Sumaini hills to link Wadi Sharm to the Mudam Plain avoiding the Ramlet Anej obstacle. Mulazim Hydra was in charge of the road-building party.

Later in the month, the post at Sba'at was fired at by pro-Saudi tribesmen. The post was reinforced and put under the command of Mulazim Hydra Shaikh.

December

There was a border incident between Sharjah and Muscat in the Wadi Madha in which two men were killed. No TOL participation in this incident is recorded.

Until this time, the terms of the Arbitration Agreement implied that the Saudi party in Buraimi could only be supplied overland through undisputed territory as were the TOL detachment. As there was no undisputed Saudi territory in contact with the edge of the Buraimi Neutral Zone it meant in practice that the Saudis would have to purchase all their supplies locally. This would clearly show the geographical isolation of the Oasis from Saudi Arabia and thereby weaken their claim to it in the eyes of the local population.

To allow a more practical method of re-supply the Tribunal agreed that Saudi aircraft could deliver to the undisputed airstrip at Kahil, and the goods collected by truck from Buraimi. This was intended to allow inspection of authorised supplies and to prevent unauthorised visitors and goods reaching the neutral zone and onwards.

On 21 December, a Saudi Arabian Airlines Dakota landed at Kahil, refused inspection and took off to land at the Buraimi airstrip without advance notice. It was unloaded quickly before being inspected, stayed overnight and departed the next morning, again without the TOL representative being allowed to check the outgoing cargo or passengers. Thereafter, the Saudi planes regularly delivered direct to Buraimi airstrip, usually with only very short notice to the TOL party there, and were unloaded secretly whenever possible.[9]

On the 24 December, Staff Sergeants Mohammed Saleh and Hassan Abdulla Noman departed for a one-year's officer training course with the Jordan Arab Army. To equip them for the very different climate there, they were kitted out with warm British Army 'battle dress' and special 'side hats' that had been sent from Jordan.

At the end of 1954 TOL were deployed as follows:

Commandant	Lieut-Col Johnson
Second-in-command	Major Smith
OC HQ Sqn/Paymaster	Captain Warner
Quartermaster	Captain Rowcliffe
RQMS	Staff Sergeant Thoma Attulla
MT Section	Staff Sergeant Playfor
Signal Sergeant	Sergeant Said Mahsin
Radio mechanic	Corporal Roberts
A Squadron	Captain Allfree
HQ Tarif outposts at Mirfa, Muqattara and Dabbaiya	
B Squadron	Captain Shaw
Sharjah, in reserve	
C Squadron (Post 1)	Captain Steggles, Mulazim Hydra, Captain Huntingdon (attached from HQLFPG)
HQ Kahil outposts at Howailat, Sba'at in Wadi Jizzi	
Buraimi (Post 4)	Captain Clayton, Sergeant Ali Azayz and 13 AORs
Tawi Husn	Section post with WS19 from the reserve squadron in Sharjah

World Events 1954

May	Indo-China	The French fortress at Dien Bien Phu fell to Viet Minh forces under Ho Chi Minh.
May	Cairo	Colonel Gamal Abdel Nasser took executive power from General Mohammed Neguib.
July	Cairo	Anglo-Egyptian agreement for British Forces to evacuate the Suez Canal Zone by the end of 1956 signed.

Notes

1 The Middle East Centre for Arabic Studies (MECAS) at Shemlan, in the Shouf Hills above Beirut, Lebanon, was a Foreign Office language school to which the Armed Services sent a number of officers each year. After three months' preliminary study at the School of Oriental and African Studies of London University, successful students went to MECAS in early January for a full year of instruction in the language, history and current affairs of the Middle East.

2 General Sir Nigel Poett KCB, DSO, at that time starting his appointment as Director of Military Operations at the War Office. He had been commanding a division in the Suez Canal Zone.

3 Both used a plain red flag, usually fixed to its pole and without any halyards or hoist.

4 A formal, traditional Arab meal, in this case after midday, at which the host would lay before his guests a huge spread of rice and goat and camel stewed with vegetables and spices. Not only would the guests be thus honoured but, when they had finished, the food would be distributed to the neighbourhood in honour of the guests.

5 When the old Imam Muhammed bin Abdullah al Khalili died, the paramount shaikhs of the Hinawi and Ghafiri groups of tribes had elected Ghalib bin Ali al Hinawi to succeed him without further consultation. This meant that Ghalib was an acceptable front for his ambitious brother, Talib bin Ali, who wanted a separate state in the interior and started to raise the tribes.

6 The Saudi 'police' party was:

Commander	Major Abdullah bin Nami, Saudi National Guard
Clerk	Abdullah Quraishi
Armed men	Musallim, Abdullah Fahad, Salim, Ali Qasir, Ta'ami (stores), Sulaiman (coffee), Mohammed Qasim (local liaison)*
Others	Ali Ali Yemeni (personal servant)
Drivers	Said Yemeni (Bin Nami's Chevrolet saloon) Marzuk Bahraini (red slat-side truck)

	Belham Hadhrami (red pick-up)
	Said Hadhrami (black pick-up)
Radio operators	Obaid Yeman,* Abdul Rahman*
Radio mechanic	Ibrahim*
Doctor	Nagi (Syrian)*
Local employees	Kenan* and Azuz* – both armed
	Sellum the cook

*Personnel retained from Turki's party.

7 Captain Robin Huntingdon MC was the HQLLFPG Intelligence Officer and had frequently visited the TOL. In 1956, having left the Army he returned to the Trucial Coast to start the Agricultural Station at Digdagga near Ras al Khaima. He became known as 'Mansur' and continued to work on agricultural projects in the 'Northern Emirates' until his sudden death in 1983.

8 Known earlier as the HUQF Force after the general area of its proposed operations. It had landed at Ras Duqum in February 1954.

9 Examination of documents captured in the Saudi camp later revealed that instructions had been sent back to Dammam that contraband and ammunition was to be hidden in sacks of rice 'to keep it away from the eyes of the British Officer here', followed by an uncomplimentary reference to myself.

7

1955

January

Heavy rain fell in the Buraimi area accompanied by a violent hailstorm over Al Ain. Hailstones about one inch in calibre pockmarked the palm-mat roofs of the TOL Post there. In the village itself a she-camel was reported to have been hit on the head by a hailstone the size of a cricket ball.

On 22 January, I heard from one of my local informants that a small caravan of five Al Bu Shamis tribesmen were on a gun-running mission into the Neutral Zone from the north. I went to Kahil that night to arrange for their interception by the TOL Squadron there. The following morning, Captain Steggles and I took a small patrol across the known camel routes through the sands outside the zone. Shaikh Salim bin Ham of the 'Awamir was camped with his wife and small son near one of these routes and I asked him to report any news of the Al Bu Shamis party to the squadron at Kahil. Shaikh Salim's little camp was in a hollow in the dunes and consisted of a shelter of sacking and canvas against a small thorn tree around which were their few essential possessions including a rifle. Shaikh Salim was a well known personality and had a small following among the scattered 'Awamir tribesmen, none of whom were grazing their camels in the area so I made the point that he should not attempt any personal heroics if the caravan came his way.

The gun-runners appeared near Shaikh Salim's camp on 24 January and he had time to send his wife and small son over the dune crest with instructions to show themselves at different places carrying sticks to look like rifles. The small boy put their milking bowl on his head as a helmet. When the Al Bu Shamis reached Salim, he persuaded them that, as there were military patrols in the area, they should hand over their contraband and make good their escape. This they did and the news reached me that evening in Buraimi. The next day I brought Shaikh Zayed from Al Ain to inspect the 21 rifles and 2,000 rounds of .303 ammunition that Shaikh Salim had captured. We found Shaikh Salim sitting on this pile of weapons that he had covered with a rug. He made little of the affair and apologised to me that he had been reluctant to demand that the five hand over their own rifles to add to the pile. The rifles were all First World War British Army .303 SMLEs that had their forestocks tapered in the Saudi manner. Recent file marks on the breech blocks had failed to remove the Saudi palm tree and crossed swords emblem that had been stamped into the metal. Some of the ammunition was still in its original cartons marked 'Special for RFC' (specially selected for the synchronised machine guns of the aircraft of the Royal Flying Corps) and dated 1916. Later the TOL came along and impounded the lot as evidence against the Saudis.

The five armed Al Bu Shamis reached Hamasa and were heard to say that they had entered the Trucial States through Dubai having come by *dhow* from Dammam.

At the end of January, B Squadron, commanded by the recently joined Major C E J Leaphard MC, Queens Bays, relieved C Squadron at Kahil.

February

Captain John Rhodes, 16th Lancers, Royal Armoured Corps, had joined and accompanied Captain Warner around the outpost locations on the routine monthly pay round.

On 9 February, a Saudi Arabian Airlines Dakota aircraft intended for Buraimi landed at Kahil airstrip in error and returned to Dhahran immediately. The next day the same aircraft arrived in Buraimi with supplies for the Saudi party.

A Squadron, under Captain Allfree, was still stationed at Tarif, with Staff Sergeant 175 Ali Azayz in charge of squadron stores.

Captain R A Laird, Royal Artillery, from HQLLFPG, replaced Captain Huntington at Kahil, who returned to Bahrain.

For some time the British officers' headdress had been the standard blue beret worn with their 'crossed *khanjar*' badge. At about this time, a two-inch square red cloth backing behind the badge was introduced.

Another development of the life of the British officers in the outstations was the arrival in the *suq* in Dubai of tins of Palethorpe's 'Ready Meal' (beef stew by another name) and 'Haricot Mutton', each tin making an adequate meal, to vary the limited menu previously available.

March

On 9 March, some soldiers deserted from Post 1 at Kahil and made their way to Hamasa, providing a useful propaganda point for the Saudis. The reason for their desertion is not known.

An Egyptian, Colonel Ali Khashaba, who had secretly been visiting Oman and the Imam, was reported to have reached Hamasa where he was hidden until he left on a Saudi plane.

C Squadron under Captain Steggles relieved A Squadron at Tarif.

Major Leaphard and B Squadron at Kahil were replaced by A Squadron under Captain Allfree. B Squadron returned to Sharjah where later Major Leaphard was relieved of his command.

An RAF Anson on its way to Buraimi with supplies for the TOL party had engine failure and jettisoned the stores over the desert, returning to Sharjah safely.

April

Major W O Little, Cheshire Regiment, joined the unit.

Staff Sergeant Ali Azayz and Corporal Obaid Salim Hiyali were sent to start training an Abu Dhabi Gendarmerie Force based at the Maqta' Fort on the landward side of the causeway. They were under the direction of Captain Steggles at Tarif and were later joined by Sergeant Abdulla Salim Neydi.

Due to rebel activity in central Oman the direct supply route through the Wadi Sumail to the Muscat Field Force (MFF) in Ibri had been cut. The MFF decided to use a route from Muscat northwards to Sohar, west through the Wadi Jizzi and turning southwards to the east of the Buraimi Zone. Their guide was a man from Ibri who led their convoy of supply trucks and troop carriers under command of Captain Ayliffe-Jones and escorted by Major Maxwell from Sohar, into the Buraimi Neutral Zone at the time of the afternoon siesta. Apparently the guide, who did not know this area, saw the red flag flying above the TOL part of the Buraimi Police camp and went towards it thinking it to be some Muscati post. As the TOL there were representing the interests of both the Ruler of Abu Dhabi and the Sultan of Muscat, it was the plain red flag, then common to both, that flew over my camp on the tallest flagpole available. The MFF party did not see the green Saudi flag on its shorter flagpole until it was too late to withdraw.

The Saudis had raised the alarm as a full company of armed soldiers was approaching in military trucks led by a Landrover with a Bren gun pointing through its windscreen and driven by a British officer. A messenger from the Saudi camp came running across to my hut calling 'Ya Captain! Ya Captain!.' I joined the Saudi Abdullah bin Nami, and we went to meet the somewhat embarrassed British officer who explained that they were lost. My attempts to brush off the matter as a navigational error and not a deliberate incursion into the Neutral Zone did enable the convoy to withdraw out of sight and continue on their way to Ibri. There was much radio traffic that night between the Saudi 'Police' and their masters in Dammam and the matter was made into a major diplomatic incident.

Passing Ma'azam, the convoy was fired on by the inhabitants and rumours of this reached Sohar, Major Maxwell's base, long before news of the convoy's safe arrival at Ibri. Major Pope, the second-in-command at Sohar, came to look for the convoy and followed their tracks which led into the Buraim Police camp a few days later. This provoked another call of 'Ya Captain! Ya Captain!' and caused further diplomatic exchanges at high level between Riyadh and London.[1]

Major Little took over from me in Buraimi on 20 April. This relief took three sorties by the RAF Valletta to bring in all the replacement stores and the Landrover that had been requested from the Quartermaster's stores over the past months. My old Post 4 Landrover, with its broken front chassis member, was driven up into the aircraft, only just climbing in before the cylinders oiled up, filling the aircraft with smoke. I flew out on the last lift to Sharjah and reported to the Commandant on Shaikh Zayed's unhappiness that he had not been consulted over the matter of my replacement. A few days later I took over temporary command of C Squadron on 29 April at Tarif from Captain Steggles, who was going on leave at the end of his first tour.

Mr Julian Walker of the British Agency in Dubai completed the first series of his researches into the internal frontiers of the Trucial States.

The British officers' headdress changed again at about this time to a plain khaki, cotton poplin headcloth worn with the *'agal* and a brooch-type crossed-*khanjar* badge (see Plate 11).

May

There were intelligence reports of a possible Saudi incursion along the coastal route, so C Squadron prepared slit trenches on the western end of the Mirfa feature. My orders were to stand in the track, wave down the advancing Saudi vehicles to stop and inform that they were about to enter the undisputed territory of the Shaikhdom of Abu Dhabi and would they please go away! Captain Rhodes had brought me these 'sealed orders' at Tarif and I was to read, understand and then burn them, which I did. We then went to the notional frontier point (see Plate 13) where we discussed how my orders would be interpreted by me in the event with the force at my disposal.

The troop at Muqattara was commanded by Sergeant Mohammad Nakhaira bin Mahroom. The Squadron Sergeant Major was Ali Salim Neyadi and Jundi Hassan Said Musharah was promoted lance corporal as the squadron clerk. The camp at Tarif was regulated by the bugle calls of the drummer boy posted to the Squadron.

The Muscat Field Force had become the Muscat and Oman Field Force and made an abortive sortie to Ma'azam from their base at Ibri. MOFF was still supplied from Muscat through the Wadi Jizzi as the Wadi Sumail remained closed to them. Later, their petrol supplies were delivered in civilian trucks from Sharjah which were escorted by the TOL to the Western end of the Wadi Jizzi. They were then taken by the MOFF to Ibri outside the eastern edge of the 15-mile radius Buraimi Zone.

The Muscati border post as Aswad was the scene of some incidents when camel caravans attempted to avoid the customs post there so the TOL set up a Post at Howailat and the Batina Force moved men to Aswad.

June

Captain Rhodes carried out the duties of Paymaster whilst Captain Warner was on leave.

Captain S G M Portal, 17th/21st Lancers, joined the force and was appointed to command B Squadron in Sharjah.

Shaikh Mohammed bin Salimin bin Rahama of the Al Bu Shamis, with 200 of his followers, were accommodated in the TOL lines in Sharjah when they came to confirm their allegiance to Shaikh Zayed.[2]

At Post 4 in Buraimi, Major Little accidentally set fire to his *barusti* hut whilst lighting his primus stove. A visitor with a message from Shaikh Zayed had mistakenly left his Landrover on the 'parade ground' that separated the officer's hut from the line of huts used by the troops and at the end of which was the radio hut. The fire from the officer's hut spread to the vehicle, which in turn set fire to the radio hut destroying the wireless equipment. Major Little was left wearing a pair of shorts. From the neighbouring Saudi camp, Abdullah bin Nami promptly offered him the use of a tent, bed and bedding and their radio set to communicate with Sharjah, all of which was refused. It is understood that Major Little spent an uncomfortable few days.

July

Captain Steggles returned from leave about 20 July and reassumed command of C Squadron at Tarif from me. I had completed my first eighteen-months' tour without a break and went back to the UK on two months' inter-tour leave. Captain Portal accompanied Captain Rhodes on the pay round to Tarif.

Captain W P Roache, Royal Welsh Fusliers, joined the unit.

Captain Rowcliffe relinquished the post of Quartermaster.

Captain Warner returned from leave and reassumed his duties as Paymaster from Captain Rhodes who took over command of A Squadron at Kahil from Captain Allfree who had completed his 18-month tour of duty.

A fire in the village of Hamasa destroyed many dwellings and the TOS escorted a relief convoy of civilian trucks with blankets, *barusti* and other supplies from Dubai over the Ramlet Anej to Kahil. This operation was intended to be a rapid response to the disaster and to make the point that such timely assistance in kind could not be provided from Saudi Arabia. Major Little in Post 4 in Buraimi was therefore instructed not to inform the Saudis until the lorries had entered the Neutral Zone and were nearing Hamasa. It appeared that the reason behind this instruction was not clearly understood for the Saudis received enough warning for them to signal Dammam, raising objections through diplomatic channels and claiming that they would provide funds for relief in cash to 'their people'. The convoy was turned back at Kahil and the supplies later used after a serious fire broke out in Deira.

In the interior, the Muscat and Oman Field Force moved again to Ma'azam, captured and destroyed the fort there, established a post of ten *wali's askaris* in the village and returned to their base at Ibri.

August

On the 9 August, Captain Laird (on loan from HQLLFPG) took over the Buraimi Post from Major Little.

September

The TOL instructors were withdrawn from training the Abu Dhabi Gendarmerie at the Maqta' Fort after the men had gone on strike because they had not been paid by the Ruler.

Whilst on leave, I was called as a witness before the Buraimi Oasis Dispute Arbitration Tribunal sitting in Geneva. Shaikh Hazza' bin Sultan Al Nahayan, his brother Shaikh Zayed, Shaikh Sultan bin Saroor al Dhahiri and Shaikh Ma'ana bin Obaid al Dhahiri also attended to give evidence at the session which ran from 1 to 17 September. Later, four of the five members of the tribunal resigned in protest at the Saudi activities and infringements of the agreement (the official statement by the Foreign Office appears on page 171).

About 27 September I returned from leave and Geneva and made my report to the Commandant. In our discussions it became clear that the removal of the Saudis from Buraimi would have to happen sooner or later. My returning to Buraimi would, it was expected, encourage the Saudis there to believe that things were 'back to normal' and my task was to foster this belief. However, I did arrange with Colonel Johnson that in the event of the TOL moving into the Oasis on such a mission, I would get from him a coded warning message at least 24 hours in advance.

I took over there from Captain Laird, arriving by the now routine Valetta aircraft and received a nice personal 'welcome back' from Abdullah bin Nami. Abdullah Qoraishi had been debarred from returning after the events in Geneva.

As my hut had been burnt down (see Plate 7) and a rough *barusti* had been put up instead, I felt that to start a rebuilding programme for our camp was in line with my orders to give an air of permanence to the place.

October

By this time, C Squadron, under Captain Steggles, had been relieved at Tarif by B Squadron, under Captain Roache, and had moved back to Kahil. Captain Portal was commanding HQ Squadron.

A Squadron, under command of Captain Rhodes, was in Sharjah.

Captain Shaw was the MTO with Sergeant Mohammed Saleh as

his MT Sergeant. WO2 CH Barnes, Intelligence Corps, was attached to HQ TOL as Chief Clerk/ORQMS from HQLLFPG.

Operations in the Buraimi Oasis

On 24 October, A and C Squadrons concentrated overnight at Burj Obaid and Kahil respectively. There they were joined by Lieut-Col Johnson and a small tactical headquarters which included Major Little. A series of false radio messages provided a deception plan that covered the movement of troops and vehicles from Sharjah.

Before dawn on 25 October, A Squadron, under Captain Rhodes accompanied by Major Smith, drove into the Neutral Zone to the joint Buraimi Police location and arrested the Saudi party with only one shot being fired (see Map 4). This was a pistol shot fired by Major Smith hitting Abdullah bin Nami in the groin. Corporal Obaid Ali Rashid was commanding a section on this operation, Ali Batti Eisa was the squadron fitter and Ismail Saddiq Othman one of the drivers.

As I had received warning of the operation, I moved my men out of our part of the camp an hour earlier on the previously announced pretext of a silent night-movement exercise on foot, leaving a shaded lamp on the track at the entrance to our site to guide the incoming force. We were to be 'left out of battle' until this part of the operation was over. I was called over to the Saudi camp by Major Smith at the request of Abdullah bin Nami who asked me to arrange safe passage for his people's personal effects. Most were in fact looted before guards from my detachment could be posted over both camps. Our camp was used as the Medical Post and also we assisted the RAF MO who had flown in on the Valetta aircraft that had landed soon after daybreak.

Abdullah bin Nami, having been treated for his leg wound as had one of his men who had been hit on the head with a rifle butt, together with the rest of the Saudi party, were flown out immediately under an armed escort commanded by Captain Portal.

Also at dawn, C Squadron, commanded by Captain Steggles and accompanied by Captain Laird, entered Hamasa from the north-west and captured Bait Turki (see Map 5). The two guards in the building hid their weapons under their beds and surrendered as soon as the identity of their attackers was known. The sound of vehicles and rifle shots brought a number of villagers into the open, some believing that it was the Saudis who had returned. The sight of Captain Steggles coming out of Bait Turki brandishing a Bren gun soon made things clear.

Leaving Sergeant Mohammed Nakhaira, Levies Abdulla Rashid al Dhahiri, Salim Said al Kaabi and another Kaabi to hold Bait Turki, Captain Steggles, with the other troop under Sergeant Nakhaira Mohammed al Jibhouni and Squadron HQ with Squadron Sergeant Major Ali Salim Nayadi, moved into Bait bin Karam and Bait Abdulrahman al Ajami nearby. Continuing the take-over of the village, Sergeant Nakhaira Mohammed banged on the door of Bait al Attar which was opened by an old lady who told him to stop making such a noise and to go away at once. She was persuaded, however, to let them in.

The vehicles that had been left in the open had come under fire from Burj al Ajam which was some way to the south-west, and another building some 100 yards to the north. The radio vehicle had been shot-up and the set destroyed, the ammunition truck, however, was collected under fire by Driver Lance Corporal Said Salim Si'ar and brought to shelter. Captain Laird's Landrover was driven on this operation by Driver Khilfan Matr al Rumaithi.

Captain Steggles attempted to neutralise the rifle-fire coming from Bait Aqeel by using the two-inch mortar firing HE and smoke bombs.

By now C Squadron was confined to the buildings by fire coming from Burj al Ajam to the west and Bait Aqeel to the north. They had lost one man shot dead, Jundi Obaid Mubarak al Katabi, shot through the head and Jundi Sayid al Hadhrami had been mortally wounded in the abdomen while climbing over a wall. He had been rescued by Captain Steggles and driven out under fire to the medical post in a Landrover by Lance Corporal Said Salim Si'ar, who then returned to Hamasa again under fire. By midday the situation had stabilised and the squadron cooks set about cooking a meal in Bait bin Karam, presumably its delivery to the troops was at times under fire.

Sergeant Mohammed Nakhaira's group left in Bait Turki were exchanging fire with Bait Rashid bin Ahmed and Bait Abdulaziz throughout that day and into the night. Their ammunition supply had run low before they discovered many sacks of rice recently delivered by air to the Saudis which contained large quantities of .303 inch ammunition. So this small party were able to keep up a remarkable intensity of fire throughout the action.

A Squadron, having been withdrawn from the Buraimi Police camp, were in reserve in the Jimi area.

The Valetta had returned bringing Mr Edward Henderson, the Political Officer attached for the operation, Captain Portal and a reserve troop of soldiers. They were met by Major Smith at the airstrip.

Tactical HQ was near Jimi from where Lieut-Col Johnson could observe Hamasa. With no radio communication with C Squadron, during the morning he sent Major Little to reconnoitre who returned to report that his Landrover had come under fire, presumably from Burj al Ajam. Accordingly, the CO decided that the reserve troop that had flown in should engage Burj al Ajam from the south, cross the *wadi* and make contact with C Squadron in Hamasa. I was fetched from where I had been helping the MO with the dying soldier and ordered to assemble the reserve troop and move to the south of Burj al Ajam. We were to neutralise the enemy fire from Burj al Alam; enter Hamasa to reinforce C Squadron there; and get a message to Captain Steggles to make a situation report to me. I was myself to remain outside Hamasa and bring back the information to the CO.

In mid-afternoon this troop was driven in Landrovers into the small sand dunes south of the Hamasa *wadi* and advanced on foot to the edge of this shallow *wadi*. The vehicles returned immediately to Tactical Headquarters. The troop, moving in open order, came under long-range sniper fire from the high tower, Burj Hamasa (see Map 5) at the east end of Hamasa *suq* so one section was sent off to try to suppress this. The rest of us crossed the shallow *wadi* to one of the large mounds south-west of Burj al Ajam in the hope of being able to use our two-inch mortar to put some bombs into the compound around the Burj al Ajam tower. Due to long storage in tropical conditions, the bombs could not reach the range required.

An advance over the open ground to Burj al Ajam was not wise so I withdrew the men back into the cover of the dunes and recalled the covering section to wait until sunset when the sniper in the Hamasa tower would have the sun in his eyes. Ammunition remaining was 5 rounds per man and 15 rounds for the two Bren guns still working. All the 6 mortar bombs taken had been fired. At the beginning of the action, each man had only one 50-round bandolier of ammunition and the three Bren guns had one box of 12 magazines of 30 rounds each.

At sunset we recrossed the *wadi* and again took up our position on the mound. When it was dark enough, two sections were sent off quietly into Hamasa, one to Bait Turki and the other with instructions to join the squadron and request Captain Steggles to come to where I would be waiting by the mound. The Sergeant with the remaining section was to approach Burj al Ajam itself to see if it had been evacuated. If so, they were to occupy it themselves and signal by whistle to that effect. If not, there would certainly be an outbreak of firing in which case the section was to make its way into Hamasa like the others, whilst the Sergeant was to return to the mound with his runner and report to me.

The Burj was still occupied. The Sergeant returned to the mound and reported that he had knocked on the door, been asked who was there, replied 'Soldiers' and the shooting started. He then went into Hamasa leaving me and my runner at the mound until Captain Steggles drove out from Hamasa without lights and causing some more firing. Having exchanged reports, we parted, Captain Steggles in his Landrover back to Hamasa to await developments and myself on foot with my escort to find the Commanding Officer some two kilometres away.

After midnight at the TOL Tactical HQ, it was learnt that the Shaikhs in Hamasa together with Shaikh Saqr of Buraimi wished to surrender and were being brought to the HQ by Mr Edward Henderson. A circle of Landrovers had been drawn up with their headlamps lighting an arena about 15 metres across. Colonel Johnson was sitting in the light with Major Smith standing beside him. Shaikh Zayed and I were together watching from the shadows outside the circle when Shaikh Rashid bin Hamed al Shamisi, his brother Shaikh Mohammed bin Hamed and Shaikh Obaid bin Juma al Ka'abi, appeared and were led before Colonel Johnson.

They were asked to confirm that they had instructed their men in the village to cease firing and keep the peace. They were also given the choice of being sent to Muscat to renew their allegiance to the Sultan, or an immediate passage to Saudi Arabia. Shaikh Saqr bin Sultan al Nai'mi was not in this group as his village of Buraimi had not been involved in the fighting though he later elected to go to Saudi Arabia.

Once the three Shaikhs had made their declarations opting to go to Saudi Arabia, I was called from the shadows and told to take charge of them until they could be put on the aircraft early in the morning.

After a quick discussion with Shaikh Zayed to find a suitable and secure premises in which to hold them, I escorted my three prisoners to my hard-top Landrover. Having got all three into the back, in the dark, I realised that they were still armed with their potentially lethal *khanjars* and that my soldier escort beside me in the front seat could not have used his rifle in case of trouble. Apologising to them for any disrespect, I had their splendid *khanjars* placed on the Landrover seat beside me. As we all knew each other this was accomplished with good grace, even Shaikh Obaid bin Juma, the most anti-British of the three, saw the humour of the situation.

Together with my Sergeant Rashid Obayed Neyadi and some of our men from the 'police' detachment, we took the prisoners to a small compound on the south-west edge of the Al Ain date gardens. The prisoners were lodged in a small outhouse with a door which was closed on them. Sergeant Rashid set the guard and I went to sleep on the sand in the courtyard.

Early the next morning the three Shaikhs were taken to the airstrip, I restored their *khanjars* to them and they were flown away to Bahrain and on to Dammam. Shaikh Saqr bin Sultan al Nai'mi followed on a later flight.

The statement by the Prime Minister to the House of Commons on 26 October describes the operation (see page 175).

During 26 October, the TOL formally occupied Hamasa village to make sure that no further hostilities occurred. C Squadron was in Bait Turki and Bait Rashid bin Hamed. A Squadron was in Bait Aqeel and the houses of the northern part of the village.

The Muscat Armed Forces had been represented during the action by their three-inch mortar platoon commanded by Major Richard Anderson. Since their arrival early on 26 October, their task had been to secure the airstrip and be on call for support if required. Later that morning Colonel Johnson sent me to fetch the Muscat platoon and invite them to garrison the Qasr al Khandaq of Buraimi (see map 5). When we approached the Qasr it still contained apparently hostile armed men and there was no red flag of Muscat flying from the tower.

The Muscat platoon was halted well to the south and I went forward alone to parley. The armed men in the fort told me that they had been ordered by their Shaikh to defend the fort to the last man and the last round and that they were ready to do so. Although they recognised me, they felt unable to accept from me that, as the fighting was over and Shaikh Saqr had left for Saudi Arabia that morning, they should surrender the Qasr. They would stay put and wished to be left alone!

After some more discussion, standing on the causeway with a number of rifles pointed at me, I did get agreement that they would leave if instructed to do so by Shaikh Saqr's bailiff, Said Kamil. So, calling to Major Anderson to wait a bit longer, I drove into Buraimi, found Said Kamil and formally asked for suitable orders to be sent to the men in the fort. As Said Kamil had no messengers available, he asked me to tell the men that he, Said Kamil, had said that they were to come home. We both then broke with formality realising how ludicrous the situation had became.

I immediately drove back to the fort to deliver the message. A few moments later, the five men with their rifles over their shoulders and their small sacks of belongings, filed out of the fort, crossed over the short causeway, exchanging compliments with me, and walked off in the direction of Buraimi and home.

Having waved Major Anderson and his men into the main entrance of the Qasr al Khandaq, I went to report back to Colonel Johnson in Hamasa. On the way I caught up with the 'ex-garrison' who welcomed a ride into the village (six of us in the small hard-top Landrover).

On the next two nights each house in which TOL were billeted had an officer allotted to it to ensure that no looting took place, Captain Portal was in Bait Rashid before returning to Sharjah and HQ Squadron the next day.

By the end of October the focus of TOL activity had moved to the western area in anticipation of some Saudi reaction. A statement was issued by the Saudi Arabian Ministry of Foreign Affairs on 13 November (see page 178).

Simultaneously with the re-occupation of the Buraimi Oasis, the TOL moved to re-establish the frontiers of the Trucial States back to the Riyadh Line and to be in position to counter any Saudi Arabian reaction or further incursion. With only three squadrons, two of which were committed in Buraimi and with only one officer still with the force who had previous knowledge of the Western Area beyond Mirfa, it was Brigadier Baird who flew in with Sergeant

Salimeen Salim and a few men to the PDTC rig location at Gezira in the Sabkhat Matti by Anson on 26 October.

B Squadron, under Captain Roache, advanced westwards from Tarif on 26 October with two troops to the Jabal Dhanna line to secure the high ground on the track. One troop remained at Tarif. The following day, as the only officer still with the unit with knowledge of the western area, I was told by the CO to fly by Anson from Buraimi to Tarif. There I had arranged to meet one of B Squadron's Land-rovers and drove to join Captain Roache at sundown on the Jabal Dhanna Line. From there the following morning I took one troop from B Squadron in two Bedfords and two Landrovers to Gezira. We met the Area Superintendent of the PDTC to discuss the logistic assistance that we required and went on to the seismic Party 5 camp at Sila as quickly as possible. This was to be the base for motor patrols up to and along the Saudi Arabian frontier (see Map 3).

The B Squadron troop, under command of Sergeant Suhail Mohammed al Gaz, that afternoon pitched camp at Sila whilst one section, under my command in two Landrovers and two Bren guns, patrolled under the scarp from the coast near Sila southwards to beyond Sufuq and to the south-west over the border in search of fresh vehicle tracks entering the territory. None was found.

The patrol returned northwards and at sundown rested at the bottom of the scarp onto the Mijann. As the old tracks had been wiped out by over a year's weathering, there was some doubt about the actual point of ascent. I reminded Driver Salim Awadh, who had been my batman in the old A Squadron days, that there had been a white stone we had used as a landmark previously. Driver Salim observed that 'the Captain was sitting on the white stone in question'. When we had cooked and eaten, the orders for the next part of the patrol were given.

Without lights and having disconnected the brake lights, which would have given away our presence, the patrol went up onto the gravel and searched along the main track until they were near the old Post 5 Nakhla site. This was a likely place for any Saudi force reacting to the events in Buraimi to seize so, at about midnight in the starlight, the two Landrovers, each with a Bren gun loaded and ready, approached the old camp site in open order quietly and in second gear.[3]

It was just possible to see dark shapes where the camp used to be. The 'battle drill' was simple, Driver Salim Awadh was to switch on his headlights at the target area when I did so. Thereafter, if battle were joined, orders could be shouted from one car to the next. When the headlights were switched on, we recognised the dark shapes as the old drums that had been used to build the Post. There was nobody there. We advanced a few more miles without lights and turned off the track to find dead ground, invisible from the main track, in which to lie up until dawn.

The first RAF aircraft that the patrol saw was an Anson that came along the track from the east quite early in the morning. The patrol had by this time returned to the old Nakhla site expecting such a visit and had concealed themselves and their vehicles amongst the old oil drums. This was both to test the effectiveness of our camouflage and as an operational precaution should there be any Saudi aircraft about.

The Anson approached at about 500 feet altitude and circled the position at a safe distance unsure of what was there. We emerged, displayed our recognition panels and waved. The aircraft replied by rocking its wings and circled lower so that Brigadier Baird's 'red hat' could be seen at the cabin window before it climbed away for Bahrain. Ground-to-air recognition signals had been agreed by myself with the Anson crew on the flight from Buraimi to Tarif some days before.

Large, black four-engined Lincoln bomber aircraft from Bahrain had been patrolling the western areas since the start of the operation, at first en route to Buraimi where they flew over the villages. Now they were concentrating on the frontier regions. The TOL patrol, in two British Army sand-colour Landrovers, had yet to establish 'friendly relations' with these heavily armed aircraft (20mm automatic cannon and .50-inch machine guns). Even so these colours did not initially bring a friendly reaction from the first Lincoln we met. However, our ground-to-air recognition panels were seen and the Lincoln flew past very low with all its guns at full elevation and the gunners waving.

November

The remainder of B Squadron moved forward to Gezira and set up its base to the west of the PDTC site. The squadron came under my operational command from Sila. A third Landrover and later a No 19 wireless set and a VHF ground-to-air set were borrowed from the oil company. Soon after this, canvas spare-wheel covers painted with a white spot in a red ring were made for recognition from the air.

The TOL were discussing being renamed Trucial Oman Scouts. On the VHF radio to the RAF I therefore adopted the callsign TOSCA which seemed appropriate. A very close relationship was established between the Lincoln crews and our patrols through this radio link.[4]

Now with three vehicles, one fitted with sand tyres, patrols were able to reach all the border areas to within sight of Sauda Nathil and into the 'Udaid peninsula, lasting up to three days at a time. I varied the routes and timings of patrols to try to create the picture of more than one unit operating in the area.

A patrol would return to Sila camp in the morning, the drivers would refuel and service the vehicles, the section of soldiers would be changed for fresh troops and the new team move off in the late afternoon to find a hide-out on the plateau for the night where they could see and hear any vehicle movement from the west. The drivers and I rarely slept in camp until the arrival of another three Land-rovers. At dawn we would move as fast as possible without raising dust, probably off the tracks, which were dusty, into the dunes near Uqlat Nakhla where we would drive up onto the top of the large dune there and stop for some time to make sure of being seen. We would move off down the slip face of the large dune into the small dunes below and move fast through them, keeping in the valleys to reappear many miles away (see Plate 1).

On one patrol, we found fresh vehicle tracks some distance inside the Saudi border. Corporal Sari was the section commander on this patrol and, by his extraordinary camel-tracking skill, estimated that they were only a few hours old. Their direction was established after following them for some distance and as they were heading east we set off in pursuit. The tracks appeared to be of one vehicle of the size of a Dodge Power-Wagon and one other smaller vehicle, perhaps a pick-up truck.

A single Saudi Dodge Power-Wagon had reached Buraimi about one year before so this little party was highly suspect. Their tracks headed eastwards keeping up on the gravel and here and there the party had stopped and circled. They were followed eastwards until the *wadis* cutting into the gravel plateau made them head more to the north-east until they were running along a wide strip of gravel that would lead to the main track to Sila. My patrol was moving as fast as we could without raising a dust cloud and as fast as the borrowed Landrover, which had a worn big-end bearing, could go.

We spotted two vehicles, one grey Dodge Power-Wagon and one red pick-up, about two miles away to the north-west having turned down off the gravel and crossed a couple of rough *wadis*. They did not look military and seemed to be heading back and away from the territory. I led my patrol onto the main track, turned to follow the intruders to make sure that they did in fact leave. They had seen us and were making all haste as their dust cloud showed. We followed them to the edge of the scarp overlooking Khor Dhuwain and down into the low dunes at its foot, where the two vehicles lost their way and doubled back and forth until they broke through onto the flat ground beyond. We returned to the top of the scarp to watch the dust cloud move away towards Uqlat Nakhla, having gained useful experience in following and analysing vehicle tracks.

By the end of the month, five TOL Landrovers were at Sila, four of which were 'gun-wagons' that had simple pintle mountings made by the local oil-company blacksmith on the tailgate for the Bren guns and simple wooden frames to locate jerrycans and the boxes of Bren magazines (see Plate 1). Two of these vehicles could be on patrol and two on stand-by, with their drivers resting. The troop had three Bren guns until a worn out Drill Purposes (DP) gun was refurbished and put into service. Usually this gun was left in camp for its defence while two or three 'good' guns went with the patrol.

'My' borrowed oil-company Landrover had by then been returned but its special wheels and sand tyres (900 x 15) had been transferred to my TOL vehicle, which also carried the borrowed No 19 set and VHF set on a large wooden board fixed behind the bulkhead. The air-to-ground recognition panels and flares were in a box on the front bumper. An old, long baseplate two-inch mortar was mounted rearwards in the back and a forward pintle mounting for a Bren gun was on the left hinge of the bonnet. On sand tyres this vehicle led the others over every type of terrain on both sides of the border from the frontier with Qatar as far south as 52 East 23 North (see Plate 16).

These patrols developed the drivers' skills in all types of terrain as well as teaching tactical drills for the use of armed soft-skinned vehicles in that desert terrain.[5]

The tactical drills evolved were primarily for the drivers and were based on their knowledge of their vehicles' capabilities with different loads aboard and their 'eye for country'. The vehicle crews' tasks were to observe in all directions, including the sky, to report anything seen, to leap out and to push instantly on the driver's order. The driver's responsibility was to get the vehicle to the next indicated objective by a route that he would select himself. The vehicle commander's tasks were the control of the crew's observation and firepower. On good going, movement would either be in line astern, with each vehicle creating as little dust as possible, keeping out of the others' dust and following on the tracks of the vehicle ahead, or in open order, in arrowhead formation, on either side of the leader.

This formation was developed for the three-vehicle patrols when using ground tactically so that the commander in the centre would advance the next bound to the ridge ahead and halt in a position to observe forward. After an interval of one minute, unless signalled otherwise, the two flank cars would move forward and reverse into position on either side of the lead car, stopping when the gunner in the back brought his gun to bear on the ground ahead. The gunner would signal to the driver silently by tapping on the driver's head to keep moving with a harder final tap to stop. By reversing into position, the gunner's head and the gun muzzle were the first things to show over the crest.[6]

On *sabkhat*, the lead vehicle lays down the track to be followed if it gets through, as in a minefield. The rest follow exactly in the tracks and help to pack down the ground for all who follow.

In the dunes, the opposite is the rule: following drivers should follow the general line of the earlier tracks noting where the going is soft and hard and choosing their own line through. The sand disturbed by the lead vehicle, even on 'hard' dune sand, is likely to be very soft. At the halts, it should be a rule that the crews walk away from their vehicle to the side and never walk in front of where it stands, again, to avoid making 'puddles' of soft sand.

Except when moving in 'bounds' tactically in dunes in contact with the enemy, when it is essential that there should be as little delay in the follow-up as possible, the following vehicles should be at least five minutes travelling time behind the leader if he is not clearly in sight. This is because the leader may be stuck in soft sand out of sight just over a ridge and needs time to get away. Although this may mean that the following vehicles sit and watch the leader getting his vehicle in and out of trouble without help, it does allow them to carry additional loads on the easier route found for them.

November

Major MacDonald returned to the TOL for another tour and went to command the Buraimi area. Shaikh Shakhbut, the Ruler of Abu Dhabi, had given the Jahili Fort to the TOL to restore and use and it was appropriate that the task fell to Major MacDonald who for so long had been in command there. This gift to the force was most likely to have come about as a result of the conversation the previous year between myself and Shaikh Zayed. The repairs and refurbishments were to be paid for out of the money captured from Bin Nami and found in Bait Aqeel.

C Squadron, under Captain Steggles, was camped at the airstrip to the east of Al Ain. A field telephone line laid between the Jahili and their camp was frequently cut, presumably by passing *bedu* who appreciated its usefulness.

Captain Portal and some of B Squadron built a mainly tented camp astride the main coast road under the western cliff of the Mirfa feature. This had been a troop location and was being expanded to house the fourth squadron being raised.

December

The patrol group in the west were officially known as Clayton Force and had their own signal net; the static base station at Sila, manned by Signaller Ahmed Juma, with exceptionally high antenna masts of small-diameter pipes I had scrounged from the oil company and each held up by two sets of guy wires. Their height was over 100 feet and so aligned that, by good fortune, the major radiation lobe on the TOL command frequency pointed to Sharjah and the lobe for the frequency used between HQLLFPG and Sharjah pointed roughly towards Bahrain. Signaller Ahmed Juma was thus able to communicate with both HQs by Morse. My Landrover carried the borrowed No 19 set and I could communicate with Sila from wherever the patrol had stopped, again by Morse, using the rod antenna.

The concept for operations in the west was that ground patrols would locate and shadow any incursion and call for air strikes from Bahrain. Should the Lincoln be in the area, or have spotted the incursion, it would take over the task of airborne strike control for the Venom ground-attack sorties. A succession of RAF pilots from the Venom Squadron based in Aden were attached to Clayton Force as Air Liaison Officers (ALOs) to 'talk the aircraft onto their targets'.[7]

A live firing exercise was carried out by two Venoms from Bahrain attacking the old oil drums at the old Nakhla camp site with 20mm cannon fire. They had been called up by radio to be there at a pre-arranged time when the spectators would be in an area marked out by recognition panels. Many hits were scored and the TOS and the oil-company spectators there were suitably impressed with the firepower on call (see plate 2).

An ARAMCO party was reported to the south and south-west of the Liwa in the area of Shatfa. A number of options were considered to deal with this, including air-landing a party of TOL nearby in an Anson. The problem was complicated by the need for the TOL to be able to support the Muscat and Oman Field Force waiting at Fahud for the arrival of the Sultan from Salalah in Dhofar on his way to Nizwa, Ibri and Buraimi. A party of one officer and 20 troops were standing by to drive to Fahud and be responsible for the defence of the airstrip whilst the MOFF advanced to Nizwa. In addition, the TOL reserve squadron in Sharjah was to remain on call. In the event, no TOL were involved in the Sultan of Oman's journey until his meeting with Shaikh Shakhbut in Buraimi and Al Ain on 22 December when the local TOL commander was present.

Captain Steggles handed over command of C Squadron to Major MacDonald and returned to Sharjah. To counter further Saudi or ARAMCO incursion into the Liwa, Captain Steggles was to prepare to re-establish the post at Humar. It was planned that he would take a TOL Landrover and be escorted by hired PDTC Dodge Power-Wagons setting out from Tarif. The Landrover was to be used for local patrolling from Humar and its petrol would be delivered by camel caravan from Mirfa. A party of 30 Levies, mainly from the Manasir and Beni Yas tribes from the Liwa area, was assembled in Sharjah but there were delays.

At the same time, a small Landrover patrol operation was being planned to go to the southern part of the Sabkhat Matti and approach the Liwa from the west in the area where the ARAMCO party had been reported. Major M E Budd, Royal Artillery, and late of the Sudan Defence Force, had recently joined and was to lead the patrol with Staff Sergeant Emil Gosous as the leading driver. They were to start from Gezira.

The RAF Lincoln aircraft from Bahrain continued to patrol the entire frontier with Saudi Arabia, flying two reconnaisance missions each day.

At the end of 1955 the TOL were deployed as follows:

Commandant	Lieut-Col Johnson
Second-in-Command	Major Smith
Adjutant	Captain Roache
ORQMS	WO2 Barnes
Quartermaster	Captain (QM) J W Stocks DCM, Royal Artillery
RQMS	WO2 Thoma Attallah
Paymaster	Major Warner
HQ Squadron and MTO	Captain Shaw
MT Sergeant	Staff Sergeant Playfor
OC Workshops	Captain S E Papworth, REME
A Squadron	Captain Rhodes at Sharjah, in reserve Captain Steggles preparing for Liwa
B Squadron	Captain Portal based at Gezirah less one troop forward at Sila under direct command of Captain Clayton, and one troop at Mirfa, RAF Air Liaison Officer attached. Major Budd to take over command of B Squadron on return from patrol to the south
C Squadron	Major MacDonald based at the Jahili in Al Ain

Captain J C M Ansell, 13th/18th Hussars, as Training Officer, Captain H A Roden, Royal Army Service Corps, as Adjutant and Captain T M (Pat) Cosgrove, Royal Army Service Corps, as Transport Officer, all arrived on 23 December.

World Events 1955

February	Moscow	Nikita Khrushchev became leader of the USSR.
November	Cyprus	State of Emergency declared in response to EOKA movement.
December	London	Britain and Egypt granted independence to the Sudan, which had been their condominion since 1898.

Notes

1 These incidents may have contributed to the lack of reaction by the Saudis to a later approach by a TOL convoy.

2 It is not clear why they needed to go to Sharjah from Qabil when Shaikh Zayed lived in Al Ain. It is certain that this number of armed men would have been discouraged by the British authorities from entering Al Ain in the Buraimi Neutral Zone for this purpose and contravening the terms of the Arbitration Agreement.

3 These Landrovers were right-hand drive so with right-handed Bren gunners the weapons' bipods rested on the centre line in the wells of the spare wheels on the bonnet. The guns were well positioned to fire in the forward arc with the maximum protection for the gunner.

4 On the map, 'Trucial States and Oman' 1:100,00 Series K668, Sheet NG–38–158, Edition 1-GSGS, Grid Zone Designation 39R, at map reference 5271, is a feature called Clayton's Ridge so named by the RAF during this period.

5 These techniques had been first recorded in the Western Desert of Egypt by the Light Car Patrols using Ford Model 'T' cars in 1916, then adopted by my father, using Ford Model 'A' pick-ups of the Egyptian Desert Survey Department in the 1930s, and put into practice by him in his operations with the Long Range Desert Group in the 1941 Western Desert campaign. They were passed on to, and learnt by, myself who was now able to relate them to this present task.

6 With a vehicle as small as a short wheelbase Landrover, the tactical problem with a front-mounted gun is that the vehicle radiator can be the first part exposed to enemy fire, but this has to be the commander's risk in the leading vehicle. On larger vehicles that are less crowded with men and their kit, the centre-gun mounting has some advantages.

7 With one notable exception, they preferred to remain in the oil-company mess at Sila after coming on their first patrol in open Landrovers. The exception was Flying Officer David Campbell who insisted on going on every patrol and even commanded a one-day patrol when I was unable to do so through illness.

8

1956

January

Officer Cadets Mohammed Saleh and Hassan Abdullah Noman returned from Jordan having successfully completed their officer training course and were appointed to Kaid's Commissions as *mulazim thanis* and went on leave.

On 5 January, a patrol from Sila searched the 'Udaid peninsula throughout its length and found neither new tracks nor signs of recent activity.

Bahrain instructed that the TOL patrol to the south-western part of the Liwa under Major Budd was not to approach within one mile of the ARAMCO party. The patrol reached the frontier in the Al Maghrib area, made a sweep along the frontier and returned to Gezira before going back to Sharjah.

Major F E Bardell TD, Royal Artillery, and Captain R O G Wood, Queen's Royal Irish Hussars, arrived at about this time. As an introduction to the unit, Captain Wood went on a patrol from Sila with me to the large sand dune above the Uqlat Nakhla. It was his first experience of being driven down the steep face of a dune which 'sang' as our Landrover descended. I learnt later that this dune had earned the name 'Clayton's Folly'.

On 28 January, in Sharjah, the troops waiting to garrison the Liwa walked out in protest at the arrest of one of their number connected with the escape of a prisoner. About 30 Manasir and Bani Yas left camp saying that they wished to leave the Levies. The Commandant was away from base at the time but returned and agreed to their immediate discharge. It was later found that the real cause of their discontent was anxiety about the safety of their families in the Liwa caused by Saudi radio propaganda.

This incident emphasised the need to fill the recently approved appointment of a Political and Intelligence Officer. The job specification was for an officer who had practical knowledge of the area, language and its people, gained over at least one tour of service with the force.

Three Dodge Power-Wagons were authorised to be borrowed from the oil company to take the Liwa garrison under Captain Steggles into Humar.

An urgent request was also made to the War Office for the issue of 20 sand tyres for Landrovers. At various times since the end of the Buraimi operation, senior British staff officers had made their winter tours of the Gulf and visited the TOL. Many of them had landed at Sila airstrip on their way back to Bahrain to see Clayton Force, often disrupting my patrol programme. Some advocated the use of armoured cars, or armouring the Landrovers, 'as we do in Cyprus', until I explained to them that the problems were not those of protection from enemy fire but the greater danger of getting stuck when in contact with the enemy. The answer was the provision of sand tyres to enable the patrols to make use of the terrain both for observation and cover from fire.

On 21 January, the Commander-in Chief Middle East Land Forces went to Sharjah and visited the TOL there. He was not one of those to visit Sila.

February

The Local Defence Committee in Bahrain agreed to the retention of the British troops in Sharjah until May and confirmed the Senior Royal Air Force Officer Persian Gulf's (SRAFOPG) intention to station Venom fighter ground-attack aircraft in the area as a strike force to meet any Saudi incursion.[1]

An exercise with the Venoms took place soon after in the western area. From my patrol Landrover, I called up Signaller Ahmed Juma at Sila and passed him the practice air-strike request in Morse code (see Plate 16). Signaller Ahmed then broke into the Bahrain-Sharjah command link to relay the message to Bahrain. The two Venom aircraft took off immediately. The pilots were briefed in the air and were called up on VHF radio by the patrol when on their descent to the target somewhere in the Mijann. They reached their target one hour and thirty seconds after the patrol's request had been received in Sila. The ALO with the patrol directed the aircraft onto their targets. After a brief discussion on the VHF radio, the pilots had to return to Bahrain. The effective 'time-over-target' available was only five minutes at that range from Bahrain (see Plate 20).

On 11 February, I handed over the patrol duties in the west to Captain A W Fordyce MC, Cameronians, who had recently joined. All operations in the western area then came under A Squadron, now commanded by Major Budd at Gezira with Captain Portal as second-in-command and to which an Army Ground Liasion Officer from the Venom Squadron was attached. 'Clayton Force' no longer appeared in the Middle East Command Order of Battle.

On my return to Sharjah from Sila I learnt that I had been selected for the job of Intelligence and Political Officer of the TOS, in preference to Major MacDonald who was as well qualified. I was provided with a Landrover and driver; told to set up an office in the end of a disused barrack hut and a field telephone direct to the CO's office was installed in it. One of the boy 'office runners' was allocated to my office and that was it. In time my duties became that of a 'universal aunt', ranging from dealing with individual *jundi's* requests for compassionate leave to taking patrols out to settle minor inter-tribal problems and visiting all the Rulers on behalf of the Commandant when he was not available. In addition, I was responsible for collecting, collating and disseminating the military and tribal intelligence that came my way. This meant writing monthly Intelligence Reports for the Commandant to submit to HQLFPG in Bahrain and attending periodic LIC meetings.

A further two officer cadets, Rashid Mubarak al Hiyali and Faisal Sultan al Qasimi, left for a one-year officer training course in Jordan.

It was decided that a fifth squadron of the TOL should be formed together with an increase of 50 per cent in the strength of the rifle squadrons. Local recruiting was stepped up. This action was confirmed by the Treasury on 15 February.

To implement this decision the training squadron was re-formed in Sharjah under Captain Ansell and moved to the Wadi Qaur later in the month. It was staffed by one of the ex-APL *mulazims*, Mulazim Thani Hassan Abdullah Noman and four local Arab sergeants. The accommodation in the Wadi Qaur consisted of one 180-pounder tent for the radio and *barusti* huts for all ranks. There was one Landrover and a Bedford with drivers, one No 19 radio set with its operator and one local donkey, employed with its owner to collect the camp's water.

The site was cleared of rocks to provide a drill square, lacking in the previous TOL posts there, and a rifle range was marked out some distance down the *wadi* to the south.

Recruits who completed their first two weeks' training in Sharjah went to Wadi Qaur for four weeks' basic training in squads of about 24. Fresh recruit squads arrived every two weeks so the average numbers in the camp were between 40 and 50. The programme covered drill, weapon training and infantry section tactics.

There had been a semi-permanent post at Tawi Husn for some years. When used it was within walking distance of the good water at Tawi Husn and able to observe the Jabal Faya track junction to Muscat and Buraimi. Its purpose was to provide a 'presence' on this important defile where main routes joined. Depending on other circumstances, this post had either a Morris truck or a wireless station for communication. In time, because of the security the post provided, a civilian coffee shop and canteen was set up by an enterprising individual to provide for the passing traffic.

On 18 February, it was proposed that the TOL be renamed the Trucial Oman Scouts. This was to bring the English connotations more into line with its new role and to appeal more to the British volunteers. The name in Arabic did not need to change.

Captain P J Adams, Royal Irish Fusiliers, joined the TOL as one of the training officers in Sharjah with Captain Roache from A Squadron (see Plates 24 and 25).

In response to recurring reports reaching HQLFPG Bahrain, who envisaged a Saudi paratroop threat to Buraimi, it was agreed with the Muscat Armed Forces that the TOL would be responsible for the defence of the whole of the Buraimi Oasis with the MAF in support. Should however the TOL Squadron be withdrawn to meet a threat from the west, the MAF would take over responsibility and the Oasis come under command of the Batina Force from Sohar.[2]

The Batina Force, commanded by Major Maxwell, already had one company in the Buraimi Oasis at Bait Aqeel in Hamasa and a detachment of 25 in the Qabil and Hafit area. Its responsibility covered the northern frontier of the Sultanate including Aswad, Mahadha, Buraimi, Wadi Jizzi, Qabil and Hafit.

The Muscat and Oman Field Force, under command of Major O'Kelly, had their HQ at Ibri and covered their western frontier area from Dhank through central Oman and down to the Sharqia. One squadron with two field guns were at Nizwa, one troop was at Fahoud and one squadron, less one troop, was in Qabil in the Sharqia.

The Muscat Infantry, under Colonel Waterfield, was based at Bait Al Falaj in Muttrah and was responsible for the coastal area from inclusive Masanah and Rostaq to Ras al Hadd and inland to the watershed in the Wadi Sumail. One platoon was deployed to Bid Bid and another in Ras al Hadd; the remainder were in Muscat together with two howitzers.

March

The Trucial Oman Levies (Amendment) Regulation 1956 dated 1 March 1956 officially changed the name to Trucial Oman Scouts. In addition, the role of the unit was amended as follows:

1 The Force may be employed in any part of the Trucial States:
   a: for the maintenance of peace and good order in the Trucial States
   b: in providing an escort for British Political Representatives
2 The Political Resident shall have power to require members of the Force to proceed and serve outside the limits of the Trucial States Order 1956

The second paragraph indicates unit's 'strategic' role envisaged by the War Office in addition to the 'internal security' function for which the Foreign Office had responsibility. This marked the beginning of the 50/50 contribution by the War Office to the funding of the TOS that brought a number of unforeseen problems. To those on the ground, the paragraph meant the possible deployment of the force into the border regions, where frontiers ran through jointly held areas such as the Buraimi Oasis, as a retrospective clause to cover the past actions at Hamasa and Khatwa on Sultanate territory. In the distant War Office, however, the unit was to be counted as a substitute for British troops able to operate throughout the Gulf region.

The design of the unit's badge was changed by the addition of two cannon barrels under the two crossed *khanjars* on a scroll with the name in Arabic (*Quwat Sahil Oman*). The new badge was worn as a headdress badge by officers but the troops kept the single *khanjar*, as did the unit flag and vehicle sign. In addition, officers wore small single *khanjars* on the shirt collar lapels (see Plates 37 and 38).

The company of the Kings Royal Rifle Corps (KRRC) from Sharjah was airlifted to rejoin their battalion already based in Bahrain in response to local trouble.

In Bahrain, their intelligence reported that a number of American M41 Bulldog tanks had been delivered to an east-coast port in Saudi Arabia. As the TOS had no anti-tank weapons, this report was of some interest but it was later learnt that the spares required for prolonged operations with these tanks were being withheld.

On 10 March, a section patrol from A Squadron in three Landrovers, led by myself, visited both Masafi villages in response to information that there was renewed friction between the two villages of that name. The southern village belonged to the Ruler of Fujairah and the northern to the Ruler of Ras al Khaima. The basic dispute was over the stream that ran through both villages whose inhabitants would take up arms and man *sangars* on hills opposite each other until someone came along and made peace between them. The TOS patrol reached Masafi by the usual route through the Wadi Siggi from the south (see Plate 9).

The purpose of this small operation was to demonstrate that the TOS could react quickly and professionally anywhere to forestall or quell breaches of the peace. The troops taking part were smartly dressed in best uniform but were fully armed and carried the section Bren gun. As Masafi could be reached by only one route through the Wadi Siggi, a 'text-book' approach in potentially hostile mountain territory would have required leaving men in picquet positions to secure the return route. A whole squadron would have had to be deployed to get one section to the objective. As this was out of the question, to avoid the technical risk of ambush I decided to return by a different route, not reconnoitered but said to have been used once by the Ruler of Ras al Khaima. Progress in the upper reaches of the Wadi Siggi followed the stream bed where the water was flowing, often with large boulders and deep pools. To get the Landrovers through, the shortest member of the patrol led on foot; where he could comfortably wade, the vehicles could follow. There were 12 men in the patrol: three drivers including myself, and nine others. With one man leading, this left eight men to walk beside the leading car, two men at each corner ready to lift it over large boulders when it grounded and to fill in the larger pools with rocks. Once out of the stream bed, the way followed the camel path up hill to the watershed. Near the top there was a gap in a small rock spine on the side of a hill. The surface was loose scree and the Landrovers slipped sideways but again, by concentrating all the muscular effort on each car as it came through, the obstacle was overcome. Once the top end of Wadi 'Asima was reached, we had no further difficulties. The patrol spent one night in the *wadi* and then returned to Sharjah, visiting Idhan on the way (see Map 2).

April

Captain C H Binns, RAMC, joined the TOS as its first Army Medical Officer and set up the medical centre. Lance Corporal Ibrahim Faraj from Sharjah was the first medical orderly to be trained by Captain Binns. Boy soldier Ali Rashid Kuwaiti from Al Ain was one of the earliest to volunteer for medical training.

Among Captain Binn's duties was the supervision of periodic disinfestation of the barrack huts from bed-bugs, which sheltered in the palm-matting walls and in the ropes of the *charpoy* beds themselves. These bed-bugs remained hidden by day but after 'lights out' emerged to crawl over the men in their beds. The Duty Officer could gauge the severity of the infestation by the number of barrack huts that refused to turn out their lights and the number of men choosing to sleep outside. Known as *qitt*, they were an unforgettable part of the soldiers' life in Sharjah. The occasional wandering bed-bug could be found in the concrete and coral buildings of the rest of RAF Sharjah, including the RAF Officers' Mess sleeping quarters, and they were probably among the original inhabitants of the Second World War Levies Camp when it was first built.

The patrols by the Lincoln aircraft over the territory were reduced to one per week, throwing more responsibility on the patrol group, still commanded by Captain Fordyce, who had now moved to Dhuwain from Sila together with the Seismic Survey Party 5. A small airstrip had been laid out on the *sabkhat* some distance from its camp. I got a lift in a Pembroke aircraft returning to Bahrain from Sharjah, intending to visit A Squadron in the west. On the way we flew over the Liwa with a touring VIP and dropped a packet of mail, maps and cigarettes to Captain Steggles in Humar.[3] Captain Fordyce collected me from Dhuwain airstrip and the next day we drove to Gezira to see Major Budd and his squadron. I then returned alone the following day to Sharjah driving one of the squadron Landrovers that needed backloading for a new clutch, a journey of about 320 kilometres.

Mulazim Mohammed Saleh went with the Liwa camel caravan to

relieve Captain Steggles, who then came out by camel to Mirfa and returned to Sharjah. He took over command of D Squadron in which the Squadron Sergeant Major was WO2 Salimeen Salim and the Squadron Quartermaster Sergeant was Staff Sergeant Ali Hussain.

The PDTC camp at Gezira was closing down so A Squadron, under Major Budd, moved to Mirfa.

May

At Mirfa, A Squadron was relieved by C Squadron, commanded by Major MacDonald, with one troop at Tarif under Captain R Wood.

One company of the Gloucestershire Regiment arrived in Bahrain on 5 May because of unrest there.

Later in the month, there was a fight at Tarif between soldiers and the inhabitants of the village that had grown near the oil-company camp. I was sent to investigate as the Ruler of Abu Dhabi had reported the matter to the Political Agent in Abu Dhabi, Mr Martin Buckmaster. This case took some three months to reach a settlement and involved a payment of Rupees 165 (about £12.40) in compensation which, luckily for me, Shaikh Shakhbut accepted and passed to Mr Buckmaster to distribute to a dozen civilian victims, by then scattered to the Liwa. On 14 May, the Political Agency in Dubai asked me to accompany Mr Ali Bustani, the Arab Political Assistant, to Wadi Madha to investigate the alleged killing of the Wali of the Sharjah village thereby subjects of the Sultan.[4] After visiting the Ruler of Sharjah, Shaikh Saqr, to take his instructions to his nearest Wali in Khor Fakkan (see Map 2) and to collect a *rafiq* for the journey, we left in two Landrovers for the east coast early on the morning on 15 May.[5]

The route was by Jabal Faya and the Wadi Qaur, through Howailat, Aswad, Khatam Milaha, Kalba, Fujairah to Khor Fakkan, which was reached by late afternoon. We spent the night in Khor Fakkan as guests of the Sharjah Wali there and arranged to send a messenger that night into the Muscat village of Madha, informing it of the intended visit by representatives of Her Majesty's Government in the morning.

Taking a guide from Khor Fakkan, our party set off early in the morning. On the way across the gravel plain before turning into the hills, one of the civilians fired a shot at a gazelle. This was unfortunate as, when we reached a point some way into the Wadi Madha on the very stony track, we were fired at from the tower above Madha village. As the shooting was at such long range, the patrol took up their position on and around a rocky hill on the north side of the open ground some three-quarters of a kilometre from the village. I sent the local guide on foot to the village to identify us as the previously announced visitors. After his arrival at the tower the intensity of firing increased, this presumably meant 'no visitors'!

Two men were next seen to leave the tower and make an outflanking movement to the south from where one of them opened fire with a modern rifle at a range of 400 metres. As this could be dangerous to the party, the TOS riflemen up on the hill, who had a clear view of their target, asked me for permission to open fire but were not allowed to do so. Having identified the firer as the son of the Muscat Wali of Madha and himself directly implicated in the murder, the APA and I agreed that further investigation was pointless. After a shouted parley we withdrew back to Khor Fakkan without having fired even one shot.

Passing Fujairah, we called upon the Ruler in his fort to give our account of the day's events. The Muscat Wali of Madha was also visiting the Ruler but I did not embarrass our host, Shaikh Mohammed bin Hamad al Sharqi, by taking the matter beyond a simple statement of our news. We reached Dubai at about 1500 hours that afternoon to report to Mr Tripp, the Political Agent.

At the end of the month, the acting Ruler of Dubai, Shaikh Rashid bin Said al Maktum, requested help from the Political Agency to raise a police force in Dubai and asked that I be made available. As I could not be released from my official duties, I volunteered to undertake this 'part-time' in addition to my other tasks.

During May, there was an investiture at Sharjah at which awards gained during the Buraimi operation were presented by the Political Resident, Sir Bernard Burrows, on behalf of the Queen:

Lieut-Col Johnson received the OBE. (See page 156)
Captain Steggles received the Military Cross and field promotion to major. (See page 157)
Sergeants Mohammed Nakhaira bin Mahroum and Nakhaira Mohammed both received the Military Medal. (See pages 158/9)
Lance Corporal Said Salim al Si'ar also received the Military Medal. (See page 160)

June

Application was made to the War Office on 19 June for the granting of regimental colours to the unit.

British officers in Sharjah HQ were wearing a smooth red lanyard on the left shoulder.

July

On 1 July, the Dubai Police held their first muster in the courthouse on the Deira side. The date chosen was a Sunday when I had time off duty from the TOS.[6]

Major Bardell was commanding B squadron in Jahili at the time of the visit to the TOS by Lieut-Col Pat Hobart, the GSO1 at the War Office dealing with Middle East Operations (MO4). He came purposely at the height of summer to see for himself the conditions in which the TOS had to operate. We left Sharjah at daybreak for Buraimi by the Wadi Sharm truck route, arriving at Jahili at midday where he spent the rest of the day and that night. The following morning he was taken over the dunes by the camel route through Tawi Masakin and Shwaib, a route I knew well to visit Captain Ansell and the Training Camp in the Wadi Qaur for lunch. We returned to Sharjah that evening.

August

The strength of the TOS was reported to be 688 all ranks including 20 British officers and 22 British other ranks.

The Training Camp in the Wadi Qaur was closed and withdrawn to Sharjah after a flash flood that rose 13 feet in half an hour threatened the site. Captain Ansell later went to Mirfa to take over command of D Squadron from Major Steggles, whose second tour of duty with the TOS was about to end.

September

My promotion to major came through and on 18 September I took a reconnaisance patrol of one section from the reserve squadron in Sharjah to Ras al Khaima to call upon the Ruler. In the afternoon we went on to Hauran, Habhab and up the Wadi Idhan to Idhan village and stopped overnight at Tawi Suhaila. The next day, we returned to Sharjah having visited Manama, Siggi, Masafi and Dhaid.

There was discussion in the Local Defence Committee (LDC) in Bahrain arising from the long-standing agreement with the Rulers that the TOS were not permitted to operate within the towns. These towns were starting to grow and already Dubai had started its own police force. The discussion points were whether the TOS should be reduced in size and a separate Trucial States police force formed, or whether there should be a police unit within the TOS or if the Rulers could form their own police forces.

October

Major J A Gibb, Argyll and Sutherland Highlanders, joined the TOS and, after one week in Sharjah, took over command of D Squadron at Mirfa on 11 October from Captain Ansell, who then went on mid-tour leave.

Captain T Birchall, General List, joined the TOS.

Captain Portal was in command of A Squadron at Jahili, where further building was in hand, probably of the new troops' kitchen in the main courtyard.

The conditions of service for Arab other ranks had remained unchanged as a two-year contract with 14 days' annual leave only. Men completing two years away from their families and clans frequently got married at the end of their service and did not re-engage. A 30 per cent wastage of trained men and NCOs was estimated which put a greater load on the training of new recruits. The Commandant obtained authority for leave to be increased to 21 days' annual leave plus an extra 21 days at the end of each contract on re-engagement. This meant that at the end of his two-year contract, a man would get six weeks' leave before returning and without loss of rank or seniority. The measure was successful and the number of re-engagements increased satisfactorily.

The selection of the British personnel for the force had resulted in very few cases of unsuitable individuals being sent to a posting where they were not able to settle down into the working and living conditions and the climate. Those who failed to complete their tours of duty were not necessarily lacking in professional qualities but had been found 'temperamentally unsuited to service with Arab troops', irrespective of the form in which this had been shown.

On 31 October, B Squadron, under Captain Birchall, took over at Mirfa; D Squadron, under Major Gibb, moved to Baraka and were joined by Captain Fordyce when the Seismic Camp at 'Udaid closed.

November

The Suez Crisis broke at the beginning of the month. On 6 November, one troop of the TOS was sent to guard the British Agency in Dubai to free the Dubai Police to patrol the town. On the night of 7 November, there was an unsuccessful attempt to burn the wireless transmitters at Sharjah. Also in Sharjah, an attempt was made to burn the Commandant's Chevrolet car, which had been captured in Buraimi from the Saudis, at his house in the town. A petrol fire bomb was used that caused damage to the paintwork.

The two officer cadets returned early from their course in Jordan as a result of the Suez Crisis and were appointed to Kaid's Commissions as Mulazim Thanis. Mulazim Rashid Mubarak al Hiyali went on extended leave for two months and Mulazim Faisal Sultan al Qasimi was posted to the Training Wing in Sharjah to instruct recruits with Mulazim Hassan Abdullah Noman.

D Squadron maintained routine patrols in the Mijann and the Bainuna visiting Agaila and Umm al Lishtan. A hunting party from Qatar was found between Sufuq and Gezira and was requested to leave the territory.

Captain Fordyce was withdrawn from Baraka and left the TOS.

Trouble continued in Bahrain and more British troops were sent there to protect property and installations. To provide support, HQ 24 Brigade were sent to Bahrain to take over command of British troops in the Gulf. The Brigade Rear HQ was in Sharjah for lack of room in Bahrain. Some of its men were taken on Desert Familiarisation Exercises by the TOS.

It was suggested that a squadron of TOS should be sent to Bahrain for duties in accordance with its new role. This was rejected by the Commandant as being outside the TOS current capabilities and the idea, wisely, was dropped.

December

British troops with Royal Navy gunfire support carried out a practice landing exercise on Sir Abu Nair island.

The Liwa detachment came under the direction of the IO at about this time and it was planned that I should visit the area regularly by vehicle if this was possible in conjunction with re-supply and rotation of the troops.

Sergeant Ali Azayz went on the December Liwa camel caravan to take over command of the detachment from Mulazim Mohammed

Saleh. Whilst at Mirfa waiting for the camels to be loaded, I together with Sergeant Ali Azayz, one driver and the guide Said bin Qasim from the Liwa in two Landrovers with normal tyres (700 x 16), made a reconnaissance of the motor route into the Liwa. We made good progress with unladen vehicles and confirmed that, with suitable tyres, supply missions would be possible. We also found that camel-caravan guides do not readily adapt to the speed and cross-country abilities of the motor vehicle and spent the night, for which we were prepared, in the dunes 'uncertain of our location'.

Captain Birchall was in command at Mirfa at this time.

Late in December, I took Major J L Bridges, Royal Warwick Regiment, who had recently joined the TOS, and a three-Landrover patrol to Humar. All the vehicles had the new smooth tread (900 x 15) sand tyres fitted. The other drivers were Staff Sergeant Emil Gosous and Corporal Salim Awadh. The patrol carried relief soldiers for the garrison, additional fuel and lubricants for the Landrover at Humar.

After one false start we reached Humar the following day. Only once did we have to unload a vehicle at the bottom of a hollow in the Qufa dunes, carry its cargo to the top and push the lightened vehicle out of the trap. The passengers named the hollow 'Emil's Pit' in honour of the driver concerned. The techniques used by the 1955 Sila patrols proved themselves in these journeys too. As leader, I went ahead for at least five minutes' distance to find a way and to leave tracks to guide the following drivers and to show where the sand was soft, often by getting stuck and trying a better route. There were therefore many hollows in the Qufa dunes named 'Clayton's Pit' during this series of patrols.

After spending one day and one night at Humar, where it rained, the patrol returned to Mirfa bringing out Mulazim Mohammed Saleh and the soldiers on relief and continued to Sharjah where heavy rain had also fallen. Many TOS vehicles had got stuck in the *sabkhat* around Sharjah and on the way to Dubai so our route from Jabal Ali was well to the south off the track.

At the end of the year, the TOS at Headquarters Sharjah were deployed as follows:

Commandant	Lieut-Col Johnson
Second-in-Command	Major Smith
Adjutant	Captain Roden

Intelligence Officer	Major Clayton
Regimental Sergeant Major	WO1 Richardson
Chief Clerk	WO2 Barnes
Signal Officer	Captain J O Fisher, Royal Signals
OC HQ Squadron	Major A H Laing, Royal Tank Regiment
Motor Transport Officer	Captain Pat Cosgrove
Medical Officer	Captain Binns
Quartermaster	Captain Stocks
OC TOS Workshops	Major Vickers, REME
Workshops Officer	Lieutenant Edmondson, REME
Workshops Warrant Officer	WO2 Overs, REME
Paymaster	Captain Tim Wood
Training Squadron Sharjah	Captain Roache Captain Adams Mulazim Mohammed Ahmed Mulazim Hassan Abdulla Noman Mulazim Faisal Sultan
A Squadron at Jahili	Major Budd, (Captain Portal having just completed his tour)
B Squadron at Mirfa	Captain Ansell (resuming command from Captain Birchell going to Training Squadron)
C Squadron	Major MacDonald, Captain Bob Wood
D Squadron at Baraka	Major Gibb
E Squadron in Sharjah	Major Bridges
Liwa Detachment	Sergeant Ali Azayz
Other officers on strength:	Major Bardell (mid-tour leave)

World Events 1956

January	Cairo	General Gamal Abdel Nasser, dismissing General Mohammed Neguib, took full power in Egypt.
March	Amman	King Hussain dismissed General John Glubb the Commander of the Arab Legion who had served Jordan since 1930.

	Paris	French Morocco granted independence.
	Tunis	Habib Bourgiba elected the first President of independent Tunisia.
	Karachi	Pakistan declared an Islamic Republic.
April	Madrid	Spanish Morocco granted independence.
June	Egypt	British troops leave the Suez Canal Zone in accordance with the 1956 Anglo-Egyptian agreement.
23 June	Cairo	Gamal Abdel Nasser elected President.
26 June	Cairo	President Nasser nationalised the Suez Canal.
29 October	Egypt	Israel invaded Egypt.
31 October	Egypt	RAF bombed military airfields in Egypt.
5 November	Hungary	Red Army crushed popular uprising.
6 November	Egypt	British commandos landed at Port Said and paratroops landed on airfield. French paratroops landed at Port Fuad.
9 November	Egypt	Military operations in Suez ended.
21 November	Egypt	British and French forces handed over Suez Canal to United Nations.
7 December	Egypt	British and French forces withdrawn from the Suez Canal.

Notes

1 SRAFOPG Group Captain Jasper Coates was an ex-flying boat pilot who, when serving in the Gulf in the late 1930s, had identified a number of emergency airfields on the Trucial Coast riding by camel from Sharjah. He also built the seaplane jetty at Sitra in Bahrain. He knew the area and spoke Arabic and understood the problems of the TOL. He was a frequent visitor to my patrol force based at Sila and developed the co-operation techniques between the ground and air forces with us in person. At the end of his period as SRAFOPG, he retired from the RAF and joined the Muscat Armed Forces as a major to command their artillery and navy at various times.

2 The origin of these reports was never fully established as the Saudi capability to mount and sustain such an operation did not exist.

3 The packet was posted through the pilot's side window and was hit by the propellor blade, which damaged it so that Captain Steggles was smoking 'half cigarettes' until he returned to Sharjah.

4 Pronounced Mad-ha, Wadi Madha was an enclave of Sultanate territory inland between Fujairah and Khor Fakkan.

5 In addition to Mr Ali Bustani and myself, were Driver 468, orderly 1316 and Jundis 1088, 737, 817 and 1079.

6 Working hours in Sharjah were:

Monday to Thursday and Saturday
0700 to 0900; 1000 to 1300; 1630 to 1830.
Friday
0700 to 0900; 1000 to 1200.

9

1957

January

The costs recorded for the TOS for the financial year 1956–7 were £475,000 and the estimated expenditure for 1957–8 was to be £500,000. The management of the budget was under the control of the Commandant once the estimates had been agreed.

Lieut-Col S L A Carter MBE MC, Sherwood Foresters, arrived as commandant designate to replace Lieut-Col Johnson.

Captain J O Fisher, Royal Corps of Signals, had been appointed signal officer.

Captain J A Flood, Royal Inniskilling Fusiliers, joined and was appointed 2i/c D Squadron at Baraka, from where a patrol rescued a number of Baluchi pilgrims stranded on the ’Udaid peninsula. At the time of the yearly pilgrimage to Mekka, it was often the TOS's sad task to rescue parties such as this. Sometimes too late to save the lives of those put ashore by villainous *dhow* captains who pointed westwards and said ‘Mekka that way’.

Captain Roache completed his tour and returned to UK.

Captain P F Chubb, Royal Fusiliers, late of the Sudan Defence Force joined as Intelligence Officer designate and accompanied me on the January Liwa patrol. The two other drivers were Corporal Ali Nasr al Habashi and Driver Ali Nasr Ya’afai.

I was concerned on this patrol to investigate further the reports from the Liwa Post of their conversations with passing travellers returning to Oman by camel which gave authentic accounts of meetings in Dammam at which Talib bin Ali declared his intention of returning to raise his revolt again in the Jabal Akhdar in the coming summer. This information I passed at once to Bahrain in the form of an Intelligence Report with the observation that it should be treated seriously as the timing of Talib's action would be when many senior British and local officials and officers were expected to be away on leave.

February

The War Office stated that the matter of regimental colours 'should rest for the present'.

On 8 February, the Commander-in-Chief Middle East Land Forces visited Sharjah and the TOS. Brigadier Baird SAOPG accompanied the C-in-C, and noticed a wide variety of shades of khaki among the officers' headcloths. Those of the longer-serving officers had faded to a rich creamy colour which was much more attractive than the initial-issue muddy khaki. This in itself was not the cause of the Brigadier's concern which was about the unsuccessful efforts by some of the more recently joined officers to hasten the fading process. Instead of achieving the rich creamy effect desired, one officer appeared in a definitely rosy pink headcloth and another in one with a distinct green tinge. The Brigadier decreed that in future all officers would wear the red *shmagh*. Naturally, this led in time to the need to define officially the length of tassels allowed on the fringes and corners of the *shmagh*.

Major I M Craig-Adams, East Surrey Regiment, joined and went with me on the February Liwa patrol. The other drivers were Corporal Salim Awadh and Driver Ali Butti Eisa. Mulazim Rashid Mubarak al Hiyali replaced Sergeant Ali Azayz who was later promoted to be Squadron Sergeant Major of D Squadron in place of WO2 Salimeen Salim.

Major Craig-Adams was then appointed to command B Squadron at Mirfa, with Captain Ansell as his second-in-command and with Squadron Sergeant Major Suhail Mohammed al Gaz.

To investigate rumours of Saudi activity in the area of Um al Zamul, I organised a camel patrol of one section from the Jahili squadron commanded by a corporal to reconnoitre the area (see Map 2). Mounted on hired camels they had a guide provided by Shaikh Zayed. Signaller Said Sulaiman from Sharjah, who had never ridden a camel before, was also leading a large bull camel with a specially made pack saddle, carrying a No 19 wireless set, balanced by one pair of fully charged batteries. They reached Um al Zamul, found nothing and returned after 23 days having been in daily radio contact, a 360-kilometre round trip. This was a typical example of the capability, when fully briefed, of the signallers and of the local junior NCOs and soldiers of the TOS, on this type of operation.

On 16 February, recruit serial number 1500 Boy Signaller Abdullah Ali al Ka'abi enlisted. The Signals Troop was under command of Captain Fisher with Mulazim Said Muhsin, Staff Sergeant Cage, Sergeant Lawrence and Corporal Roberts, all Royal Corps of Signals, and Corporal Abdilla Salem Yaafai.

I took a patrol along the western foothills of the Western Hajjar mountains from Wadi Siggi southwards to Tawi Fili and the Wadi Qaur to seek news of Mr Julian Walker, the Political Officer researching the local frontiers whose return was overdue in the area of the watershed in the Wadi Madha region.

The TOS had received some 3.5-inch anti-tank rocket launchers and a small supply of rockets for them. My previous mission to the Wadi Madha area had not been without incident so to carry a 'bigger bang' I was about to take one of the bazookas with us, but was stopped by the Commandant who saw the weapon being put into my Landrover.[1]

Mr Walker later appeared at the Wadi Qaur Training Camp unharmed and unaware that he had been reported overdue. Throughout Mr Walker's long period working on the internal frontiers task, there is no record of the TOL or TOS being asked to provide an escort for him, however small, for which they were originally formed. It was considered that a military presence would inhibit his freedom of action.

March

Between 9 and 11 March, the 'Squadron Roundabout' operation took place. E Squadron, under Major Bridges, moved from Sharjah to Mirfa, B Squadron, under Major Craig-Adams, moved from Mirfa to Baraka and D Squadron went from Baraka to Sharjah. C Squadron was deployed at the Jahili.

The ration allowance for British ranks in outstations was reduced to 15*s.* per day after having been raised to the generous sum of 21*s.* per day about a year before.[2]

I was sent to reconnoitre the Al Khatt region and to recommend a suitable location for a new squadron base there. Preliminary arrangements were agreed over the supply of water from the wells and the local acceptability of the site on the gravel plain away from the edge of the hills and my report was made to the Commandant.

The squadron in Jahili sent a routine signal that Corporal Ali Nasr had left for Sharjah in his truck 'Old Blue'. He had not arrived by midday the following day so a signal was sent for confirmation of his departure. The reply was affirmative and that a small convoy leaving that night would pick him up. Corporal Ali always carried water and food for three days so was not expected to have come to any harm. Early the next morning, the convoy arrived without him but reported having seen him, 'actually, only his feet, under his truck in the Ramlet Anej'. Because of the soft sand there they had been unable to stop but, as 'his feet were moving', they believed he was working on the vehicle. At midday, a solo rescue mission by myself had been decided when 'Old Blue' appeared, puffing steam and grinding along, at the camp gate. There it finally broke down and Corporal Ali, grey with tiredness, got out of the cab, shut the door which almost fell off as the hinge broke, came over to the Commandant and myself, saluted and said, '*Khalas* – it's finished'.

'Old Blue' was towed to the workshops and sold as beyond economical repair (BER) a few days later. Some weeks after this, it was reported that a *bidfa* looking like 'Old Blue' was carrying the usual 20 civilian passengers and five tons of cargo on the Wadi Qaur route to Muscat.

With a small escort commanded by Sergeant Mohammed Nakhaira MM, I accompanied the PR and Lady Burrows on their visit to Shaikh Shakhbut in Abu Dhabi.[3]

Lieut-Col Carter and Major Gibb toured Ras al Khaima and Rams and the sulphur pools at Al Khatt as part of the new Commandant's introduction to the territory.

A proposal to raise a pipe band was made to the War Office.

April

I completed the hand-over of my duties as Intelligence Officer to Captain Chubb and left the TOS on 8 April, having completed two full tours of duty with the unit and having accumulated 180 days' leave before rejoining my own Regiment in Germany.

Captain Birchall was Acting Adjutant. Captain R G Barton, Royal Artillery and Lieutenant D J C Stewart, Royal Innsikilling Fusiliers, joined the force.

In London, the decision was taken to double the size of the force in an exchange of letters between the Foreign Office and the War Office. This expansion was to be in two phases over the next three years.

May

D Squadron were sent to guard the British Agency in Dubai on 6 May in case of trouble during the expulsion of an Egyptian schoolmaster.

Lieut-Col Johnson completed his hand-over of command to Lieut-Col Carter on 20 May and left the TOS after the customary dining-out party in the British Officers' Mess.

June

D Squadron under Major Gibb and Captain Flood, with Mulazim Faisal Sultan al Qasimi and Squadron Sergeant Major Ali Azayz, moved to the Jahili.

The rebel leader, Talib bin Ali, returned to Oman and landed by *dhow* on the Batina coast on 14 June, having been delayed on the way. This confirmed the information received through the Liwa Post and the related forecast in my Intelligence Report made in January to Bahrain. The Political Resident and the Chief of Staff of the Muscat Armed Forces were on leave.

Captain J W Woodruff, Royal Artillery, who had recently joined, and Lieutenant Edmondson carried out desert trials of the Austin K5 truck 1 ton 4 x 4 and a Dodge (UK) truck 1 ton 4 x 4 (not the Power-Wagon), both fitted with sand tyres. These two vehicles were used in the Dhafra and the Liwa in support of two Landrovers on a patrol looking for gun-runners. Corporal Ali Nasr Nabashi drove the Dodge, Driver Ali Batti Eisa the Austin and Staff Sergeant Emil Gosous drove one of the Landrovers. During this operation, one Landrover broke its back axle and the other its gearbox but were repaired in the field by the strong team of fitters on the patrol. The two trials vehicles failed to come up to expectations as they lacked power in the sands, again proving the case for the American Dodge Power-Wagon as used by all the oil companies in Arabia.

The Release Note for the issue of pipe-band equipment to the TOS from Central Ordnance Stores was dated 25 June, before the War Office and the Foreign Office had finished arguing over who was to pay.

July

Major Gibb went on leave on 1 July and Captain Flood assumed command of D Squadron. Captain Chubb had been promoted to major.

Quartermaster Sergeant Thoma Attallah was promoted to *Mulazim.*

Mulazim Hassan Abdullah Noman was the Arab Adjutant.

Artificer Sergeant Playfor had been awarded the British Empire Medal (BEM).

The post at Mirfa was abandoned and E Squadron was renamed C Squadron at Al Khatt.

Brigadier Baird was due to be replaced by Brigadier Tinker, late 13th/18th Hussars and Trans-Jordan Frontier Force.

Having completed their tours of duty, Captains Roden and Cosgrove together with Chief Clerk WO2 Barnes, were due to leave the TOS at the end of the month.

The following officers were reported as on their way to join the TOS: Captain P V Burnand, 14th/20th Hussars; Major W A F Maynard, Royal Hampshire Regiment; Lieutenant G A Shepherd, Royal Tank Regiment; Captain R L G Weir, Royal Army Service Corps; Captain K Wilson, Royal Scots and Captain W H Stevens, Duke of Cornwall's Light Infantry, on attachment on leave from MECAS, Lebanon.

On 16 July, the revolt in Oman broke out with the ambushing and rout of a large part of the MOFF from Nizwa near Balad Sait by Talib's men. Four vehicles were mined and lost and many troops deserted or were captured, together with their weapons including a number of Bren guns. The rebels captured Nizwa and the MOFF ceased to be an effective force.

Ordered by Bahrain to go to the assistance of the Sultanate of Muscat, the TOS prepared to move immediately. The British reinforcement plan for the Gulf was also put into action, with the airlift of the 1st Battalion, The Cameronians (Scottish Rifles) from Bahrain to Sharjah.

On 21 July, D Squadron moved from Al Ain to Ibri by the western route, well away from Dhank, Ma'azam and Sanaina, which were reported to have gone over to the rebels, guided by Douda bin Maktoom al 'Amiri, well known to the TOS and an uncle of WO2 Ali Azayz. B Squadron, from Sharjah followed up, staging at Jahili. A Squadron were withdrawn to Sharjah from Baraka where a company of the Cameronians took over. Another company of the Cameronians went to Buraimi and took over the Muscat Armed Forces location at Bait Aqeel and the Jahili from the TOS.

D Squadron, under Captain Flood, was organised as four troops with Mulazim Faisal Sultan, WO2 Ali Azayz and Staff Sergeant Ali Hussain Yafai in squadron HQ. The Troop Commanders were Sergeants Obaid Ali Rashid, Obaid Salem Hiyali, Khamis Saif Ghaithi and Saif Ahmed bin Maya from C Squadron.

A Tactical HQ was set up at Ibri the following day by WO2 Barnes. The Commandant, Adjutant, IO, and the recently joined Captain Stevens and Lieutenant Stewart arrived. The MO also went to Ibri and then on to the PDO location at Fahud to set up a casualty evacuation route, then flew back to Sharjah on 27 July.

On Saturday 27 July, there was a confrontation in Major Bridge's C Squadron at Al Khatt. Some 12 soldiers then left with their rifles and a further 14 men were demanding transport to go to see Shaikh Zayed in Al Ain. Major Smith was unable to leave Sharjah until the MO returned from Ibri late in the day. The two officers with a platoon of the Cameronians went to Al Khatt that night to be in position around the Al Khatt camp by dawn the next morning. Bren guns were on the cabs of their Bedford trucks to cover the camp. Major Smith went in and paraded those present, ordering them to lay down their arms. The real troublemakers had left long before and were eventually brought in by Mulazim Mohammed Saleh from their Shaikhs, namely Shaikh Zayed in Al Ain and Shaikh Abdullah bin Salim in Mahadha.

The cause of the trouble was disquiet over propaganda broadcasts from Radio Cairo about the events in Oman that reported heavy casualties among their comrades. The lack of information given to their British officer meant that, as they were unable to solve the problem in discussion, they demanded to see their Shaikh and hear the news from him.

Lieutenant Shepherd arrived and was appointed Signals Officer. He went forward to join the Tactical HQ at Ibri.

The Commander-in-Chief Middle East Land Forces, Lieutenant-General Sir Geoffrey Bourne, visited Ibri and explained to the troops assembled there that they would be supported in the forthcoming action by the British. At the same time, Radio Cairo was broadcasting anti-British propaganda saying that British troops were forcing Arab soldiers before them to the attack with machine guns at their backs.

This was a new situation for the TOS soldiers, whose training and operations had been within the territory of the Trucial States in static watchposts and mobile patrols. Their Bren guns and motor vehicles had given them superior firepower and mobility over local opposition, armed only with low velocity single-shot weapons and few modern high-velocity rifles. Though their tactical training had included 'fire and movement' at section level during basic training, subsequent live field-firing exercises had been section fire control in defence. Their weapons were bolt action rifles and Bren guns (the two-inch mortar was not a 'support' weapon and its ammunition was unreliable). They had not trained with grenades nor with sub-machine guns and had not even seen a three-inch mortar or a Vickers medium machine gun.

Never before had there been any reason to explain to the men that in full-scale military operations, the supporting artillery, mortars and heavy machine guns were fired from behind the attacking troops to neutralise the enemy. There was a great deal of concern about this among the soldiers due to the Egyptian propaganda. This concern was not fully understood by the newly joined British officers.

Whilst at Ibri, B and D Squadrons carried out ten days of training with the Cameronians including troop/platoon and squadron/company level live-firing exercises with the medium machine guns and three-inch mortars of their Support Company.

'Carter Force' at Ibri consisted of the Tactical HQ, B and D Squadrons TOS, one rifle company and Support Company of the Cameronians and their Battalion HQ. Rear HQ was established at the Jahili.

August

On 5 August, Carter Force had moved to its concentration area at the well at Awaifi some 40 miles towards Nizwa from Fahud and joined up with the Northern Frontier Regiment. Supplies were flown in to Fahud airstrip.

That evening the column formed up with the TOS leading, followed by the NFR and then the Cameronians and moved off. After seven hours' driving they stopped about ten miles from Izz for some rest.

On 6 August, at 0530 hours, the advance to Izz began. Approaching the village, the force moved out into open formation with the two TOS squadrons in Landrovers and Bedfords leading. Tactical HQ was in the centre and the mortars and machine guns of the Cameronians in position to cover the advance.

A reconnaisance party went forward with Major Coates, of the Muscat Armed Forces, flying a large red flag on his vehicle accompanied by Captain Shepherd in a second Landrover. Izz was not defended and the village elders came out and surrendered the village.

The force advanced beyond Izz and camped for the day while parties searched for a suitable area for an airstrip to take Valettas and perhaps Beverley aircraft. One was found to the north of Izz.

Brigadier Robertson, who had been sent to command the joint British/TOS/Omani land force and the RAF in support, arrived with his small staff. He ordered that the British troops were to be self-contained on 'light scales' of equipment, which meant doing without their tentage. Almost immediately there were seven cases of heatstroke. The TOS MO revived them by having them driven about whilst being splashed with water. In the shade of the vehicle canopies and in the very dry air, the evaporation cooled them enough for them to be evacuated by air. The British troops then adopted the TOS practice of creating and using every bit of shade and shelter from the sun.

The Venoms and the Shackleton were attacking with rocket and cannon fire only those forts and towers that were flying the white flag of the rebels.

At dawn on 8 August, the advance continued and at Radda, one of the Firq group of villages, the leading troops debussed and continued the advance on foot. Radda itself was not held and they remounted. Nearer Firq, the NFR reconnaisance party, this time with Major Chubb and Staff Sergeant Cage accompanying them, came under fire. The NFR escort abandoned its vehicle and withdrew. Major Chubb and Staff Sergeant Cage brought it back for them.

Some 300 metres in front of Radda were the first date gardens with a group of mud houses at their right-hand end. Though these gardens were still occupied by the enemy, D Squadron bypassed them and went into the second group of date gardens some 400 metres further on towards Firq. The enemy in the second gardens withdrew about 400 metres into stone *sangars* from where they opened effective fire on D Squadron. Jundi 1325 Saif bin Obaidil was hit in the chest and seriously wounded. He was rescued and brought back over a garden wall to shelter by Corporal Ali bin Sabt al Mansouri. The other two casualties were Jundi 955 Khalifa Salim Kharsoom, hit in the hand whilst reaching up to pick some dates, and Jundi 1577 Saif Salim Nayadi, also hit in the hand while carrying a spare barrel for the bren gun.

Captain Wilson and Lieutenant Stewart were on the right flank of the squadron to fire a 3.5-inch anti-tank rocket in the general direction of the village of Firq itself, at a range of some 600 metres half right from the line Radda, first and second gardens. Venoms and a Shackleton aircraft were also firing at Firq and at the enemy positions on the hill behind Firq.

The Cameronians set up their medium machine guns on a rise behind and to the left of Radda with their mortars further to the rear to give supporting fire.

B Squadron had by now moved into the first date gardens, the enemy there having hidden their weapons in their houses.

D Squadron had no radio and their medical orderly, Said al Mazroui, had not come forward in the advance to the second garden so Corporal Mussobih volunteered to take a message and ran back to the first garden and on to Tactical HQ behind Radda. He returned with Captain Binns the MO, Medical Corporal Ibrahim Faraj, a British sergeant and the squadron medical orderly, bringing a stretcher with them to the forward edge of the first garden. In front of them, the open ground to the second garden was exposed to enemy fire.

With Corporal Ibrahim and the British sergeant carrying the stretcher, the whole party ran forward under covering fire towards the second garden. The Medical Officer and the British Sergeant went to ground about half way across the open ground. Corporal Ibrahim, having dropped the stretcher, and Corporal Musobih reached the second garden. The MO and the sergeant then crawled forward to collect the stretcher and made a dash forward to the second garden. During all this, quite a lot of Vickers machine-gun fire whipped through the trees of the second garden and some three-inch mortar bombs were also dropping short close to D Squadron's forward positions.

Captain Binns, having tended the wounded as best as he could and leaving Corporal Ibrahim to look after them, offered to take a message back to the Tactical HQ. Captain Flood wrote a situation report and Captain Binns set off back at a fast run to cover the 400 metres of open ground. He came under fire from his left, so the Vickers guns opened up with covering fire from his right which passed close overhead. After sprinting for about 200 metres, he dived to the ground to regain his breath and to find some shelter from the more accurate fire now coming at him. The spectators were not sure if he had been hit but cheered loudly when a, by now, very angry

Medical Officer completed his home run. The situation report was delivered to Colonel Carter and Captain Binns went over to the Cameronian machine gunners to indicate the correct targets for the next phase.

Under covering fire, D Squadron withdrew together safely with the walking wounded and the stretcher party in their midst.

As the day had now passed and not wishing to remain in contact overnight, the force withdrew two miles to *laager* for the night near Karsha. Jundi Saif Obaidil was evacuated by air to the oil-company medical post at Fahud where he died from his wounds the following day.

There was a lull the next day whilst permission was sought from London for the RAF to use bombs and to fire upon villages. One troop of Ferret scout cars of the 15th/19th Hussars arrived by air and went into action as soon as they landed against two of Sulaiman bin Himyar's Landrovers, which they turned back from trying to reach Firq from Birket el Mauz.

Another quiet day on 10 August during which permission for the RAF to use 25-pound fragmentation bombs was received. That night the Hussars laid an ambush on the track from Birket el Mauz and destroyed one of the Landrovers that again tried to reach Firq. Colonel Carter took a reconnaisance party of the IO and the Signals Officer under cover of darkness to the Firq airstrip to see if the area was still occupied and to assess the condition of the airstrip itself. The enemy held the ridge behind the airstrip in strength and the reconnaisance party's vehicle brake lights drew their fire. It is not recorded whether this was intended.

On Sunday 11 August, Firq was guarded on its left flank by the mountain ridge, honeycombed with caves and dominating any approach to the village. The Cameronians rifle company made a silent attack on this ridge by night and the rebels, surprised, put up only the briefest resistance and withdrew. At dawn, the force occupied Firq without opposition. The Venoms reported rebels streaming back into the mountains under their attack by cannon fire.

The Hussars led the advance to Nizwa which surrendered to Sayid Tariq representing the Sultan.

The TOS made their camp beside the river below Nizwa and D Squadron placed piquets in the Nizwa and Firq forts on 12 August. B Squadron, under Major Craig-Adams, led the advance to Birket el Mauz to make contact with the Muscat Forces (Haugh Force)

ABOVE. **IO's patrol, Tawi Fili, February 1957.** The tower by the well was unoccupied. Stone and gravel cover the west of the Hajar Mountains in the background. BELOW. **Sharjah Creek, March 1957.** Looking South upstream towards the town corniche from the front steps of the TOS Officers, Mess (see Plate 28).

ABOVE. **Officers of the Trucial Oman Scouts Sharjah, October 1956.** Waiting for a group photograph. The Levies Camp hut behind used as the TOS school was similar to the rest of the barrack huts, made of rush boards with corrugated sheet-metal roofs and palm-matting veranda shades all around. One of the two cannon outside the HQ Hut is shown on the right. BELOW. **The Sharjah HQ officers of the Trucial Oman Scouts, October 1956.** *Seated left to right*: Captain Stocks, QM; Major Vickers, REME; Major Smith 2i/c; Lieutenant Colonel Johnson, CO; Major Laing, HQ Squadron; Captain Wood, paymaster; Major Clayton, IO. *Standing left to right*: W01 Barnes, ORQMS; RSM Mohammed Ahmed, Captain Binns, MO; Lieutenant Edonson, REME; Captain Cosgrove, MTO; Captains Adams and Roache, Mulazim Hassan Abdullah, Training Wing; AQMS Overs, REME. *Behind:* RSM Richardson.

ABOVE. **Mirfa Post, December 1956.** The outriders of the caravan from the Liwa post approaching from the south. The main coast track to the west runs through the Post between the tent and the white stones around the officer's hut. BELOW. **Post 10 Humar Liwa, February 1957.** A mixed group of TOS and local inhabitants on the occasion of the IO's re-supply patrol visit. Driver Ali Batti Eisa is second from the left at the back behind Corporal Salim Awadh beside Major Craig-Adams. *Standing centre*; the guide Said bin Qasim and Lance Corporal Saleh Thani Neyadi. I am sitting bareheaded talking to Sergeant Ali Azayz.

ABOVE. **The Trucial Oman Scouts Officers' Mess, Sharjah, 1959**. Until 1953, the building housed the British Political Agency for the Trucial States. Of traditional local construction, using coral and mortar with *chandal* pole ceilings, the dining room and lounge were on the upper floor and most of the bedrooms below. BELOW. **Dubai Creek, Deira side, March 1957.** The long building with the green verandah was the first municipality office. The first office of the British Bank of the Middle East was in the long low building with an opening onto Abra Square.

ABOVE. **The Officers' Mess, Jahili, March 1960.** The rooms around the central tower were built by Major MacDonald in 1956, with mess room, kitchen and bedrooms including one in the tower itself. (see plate 11). BELOW LEFT. **Footwear.** *Front:* 'Sandal, Muscat Levies' as worn by Arab other ranks. *Rear*: Clark's 'Desert Boot' British officers' working dress. *Right*: Clark's 'Chupli Sandal' British officers' parade dress. BELOW RIGHT. **Levies and Scouts shoulder titles.** June 1953 TOL pattern on left, locally made 1956 TOS pattern on right.

ABOVE. **TOS Boys Squad, Sharjah, May 1957.** Staff Sergeant Said Mahsin teaching the boys inside the School Hut (*see Plate 24*). The matting walls provided an ideal habitat for insects in the dormitory huts. BELOW. **TOS Boys Squad, Sharjah, May 1957.** Trainee drivers and mechanics under instruction by Staff Sergeant Emil Gosous (*left*).

ABOVE. **Jahili Fort, Al Ain, May 1957.** The entrance arch had been demolished and the signboard re-sited since June 1956 to improve vehicular access. BELOW. **The officers of the Trucial Oman Scouts, Sharjah, May 1957.** *Seated left to right:* Major Atkinson, QM; Major Laing, HQ Squadron; Major Budd, A Squadron; Major Smith, 2i/c; Lieutenant-Colonel Johnson, CO; Captain Birchall, Adjutant; Major Craig-Adams, C Squadron; Major Gibb, D Squadron; Captain Chubb, IO. *Standing left to right*: Lieutenant Edmundson, REME; Captain Cosgrove, Training Squadron; Lieutenant Barton; Captain Flood, D, Squadron Lieutenant Steward, Training; Captain Binns, MO. Colonel Carter took over command soon after.

ABOVE. **Officers headdress, Trucial Oman Scouts from 1957**. As worn in Plate 36. see Plate 4 for first head-gear and Plate 25 for khaki head-cloth.

LEFT. **Officers' working dress from 1956 to 1958**. Silver single khanjar collar badges and red stable belt. Leather Sam Browne worn on parade.

from the east coming through the Wadi Sumail. Among their officers was Captain Allfree (ex-TOL). This reunion of two officers from the East Surrey Regiment was fully covered by press photographers.

On 13 August, a series of joint patrols by TOS, NFR, 15th/19th Hussars, and Royal Engineers reached Bahlah, Balad Sait and Tanuf. On instructions from the Muscat authorities, the Royal Engineers started to prepare for the demolition of Sulaiman bin Himyar's fortified village of Tanuf using three tonnes of explosive.

The MO, RSM Richardson and Lieutenant Edmondson found a new kerosene refrigerator still in its packing case in Sulaiman bin Himyar's fort in Tanuf on 14 August. This was saved from destruction by being soon bolted to the floor of the workshop stores truck where it remained until its return at the end of the campaign and subsequent installation in the medical centre at Sharjah. Meanwhile, it was used for the preservation of medical supplies which, when available, included lager beer.

The demolition charges that destroyed Tanuf were fired by Sayid Tariq.

Tactical HQ and B Squadron moved from Birkat al Mauz to Izki on 16 August and B Squadron set up a tented camp outside the group of villages there. They were joined by the troop from 15th/19th Hussars.

The Cameronians' Battalion HQ and Support Company left on 17 August by road through the Wadi Sumail to the PDO base at Azaibah near Muscat on their way back to Bahrain.

On 19 August, the village forts at Izki were blown up.

During this period, the TOS camp at Izki was visited by the Air Officer Commanding Arabian Peninsula, who congratulated the TOS on the operation and awarded the Arab ranks two months' bonus pay.

The NFR started to build its new camp near Nizwa to replace the MOFF camp destroyed at Firq.

A report during this period mentioned that 'an officer of the Cameronians had died whilst with a party climbing Jabal Hafit'. The subsequent Board of Inquiry brought out that without adequate preparation, insufficient water, without a local guide and with his men dropping from heat exhaustion at midday, the officer bravely attempted to return down the mountain to get help and himself collapsed and died at the foot of the hill. This is yet another incident, this time tragic, of a British unit getting into grouble through failing to appreciate the dangers of climate and terrain and perhaps unwilling to ask the advice of the local forces experienced in such matters as movement and survival.

Major Gibb, returning from leave on 26 August, re-assumed command of D Squadron and the Cameronians personnel in Buraimi. As the Cameronian officer's body had been found by Shaikh Ali bin Ahmed al Salf of Hafit, Major Gibb arranged a presentation of a rifle in gratitude from the Regiment on its behalf.

On 27 August, the remaining TOS at Izki returned to Sharjah, Tactical HQ, B and D Squadrons travelling by road to Azaiba whence the personnel flew out, their vehicles being shipped back by tank landing craft. The TOS troops went on leave until their vehicles and equipment arrived in Sharjah. D Squadron then returned to Jahili.

Captain Ansell completed his tour and Captain Birchall went on mid-tour leave.

September

Lieut Edmondson completed his tour on 4 September.

The British Member of Parliament Mr Julian Amery, the Director of Infantry General Firbank and Brigadier Tinker visited the unit. General Firbank asked Captain Binns to give him a full report of the medical aspects of the campaign. The whole concept of training and logistics for any future British support operations in South East Arabia was changed soon after, as a result of the report.

In D Squadron, Captain Flood going on mid-tour leave was replaced by Captain C C Hammick, Grenadier Guards, who later took over command when Major Gibb was evacuated, sick, to Sharjah.

October

The TOS underwent a major re-organisation and revision of its operational and training concepts as a result of lessons learned during the short campaign in Oman. They had achieved all the aims envisaged in their original formation: caravans were no longer ambushed; people could travel anywhere within the Trucial Shaikhdoms without fear; British Political Officers could travel without escorts; there was no slave trade and the Saudis had been expelled from Buraimi with the minimum of force.

Major Gibb had previously served with the South Waziristan Scouts and had active first-hand experience of mountain warfare operations. He was selected to organise and command the new Training Centre at Manama and handed over command of D Squadron to Major Hammick (who was later succeeded by Major Maynard).

The Training Centre started work on 23 October with Captains Birchall, Burnand, Green and Wilson looking after recruit and continuation training. Mulazim Faisal Sultan was Piquet Training Officer. Captain Shepherd also had a Signals School at the Training Centre where Said Mahsin, promoted to *mulazim* and awarded the BEM, was in charge of the recruit signallers.

In Sharjah, the Signal Centre was supervised by Staff Sergeant Cave who, with four British operators, two British radio mechanics and a driver electrician, were all from the Royal Corps of Signals. Additional operators and the signallers in the outstations and with the squadrons were, of course, all Arab.

A Squadron was at Ibri under Major Budd.

B Squadron commander, Major Craig-Adams, had been evacuated to Bahrain for medical treatment so the squadron was in Sharjah commanded by Captain Turner.

C Squadron was (presumably) still at Al Khatt.

D Squadron under Major Hammick were still at the Jahili.

There was a TOS detachment at Humar.

A platoon of the Cameronians company in Sharjah was holding the TOS Camp at Baraka.

The budget for the TOS dated 28 October 1957 noted an establishment strength of 25 British officers, 12 Arab officers, 43 British other ranks and 1,186 Arab other ranks, making a total of 1,266 all ranks.

A tribal blood feud led to the murder of a minor shaikh, the murderers fleeing westward towards the Liwa. B Squadron and Colonel Carter with a small Tactical HQ went to the Bainuna to be joined by Shaikh Zayed and some of his men at Bidia where they stayed for some days in an unsuccessful attempt to discover the murderers.

From Jahili, D Squadron sent patrols out to intercept two Bani Ka'ab, reported to have been sent to murder Shaikh Abdullah bin Salem, but failed to find them.

November

The rebels in Oman had stepped up their mining of the routes with the onset of cooler weather and action to counter this had become necessary. The plan was that the NFR should make an advance up the Wadi Kamah from Tanuf onto the Jabal Akhdar supported by scout cars of the 13th/18th Royal Hussars (who had relieved the 15th/19th The King's Royal Hussars) and a composite squadron of the TOS. Venoms would also be available. (See Map 6)

On 7 November, B Squadron moved off from Jahili to Izki arriving on 10 November to set up the base camp about a mile from their old August location. On 8 November, the Commandant with Major Gibb, SAOPG and SRAFOPG flew to Nizwa via Muscat. On 12 November, Colonel Carter, the Signal Officer and Captain Green arrived at Izki. On the following day the three British officers, who were to command the picqueting troops flew over the area to reconnoitre. Their task would be to hold the hills on both sides of the *wadi* to secure the start of the route for the NFR.

The TOS composite squadron for the operation was called 'Gibb Force', after its commander, and consisted of Captain Turner with a troop from B Squadron, Captain Burnard with a troop from the Training Centre, Captain Wilson with a troop of C Squadron and four British staff sergeants recently arrived from the UK. Man-pack No 31 radio sets were now available and were carried and operated for the first time by the TOS signallers.

On 15 November, after dark, 'Gibb Force' moved off to Nizwa to follow the NFR to the mouth of Wadi Kamah where they dismounted. Their HQ was set up about a mile up the *wadi*. The two picquet troops climbed to their positions before dawn and supply parties of civilian porters had been engaged by the NFR to take up food and water during the day. The re-supply of the two picquets on the mountains either side of the *wadi* did not go smoothly as the civilian porters either turned back at the sound of firing or refused to carry their loads up the final slopes.

The NFR company assault, led by Captain Allfree and supported by the Venoms, made some progress under fire from rebel positions and by nightfall had reached within 500 feet of the summit.

The NFR were expected to put in a night attack but instead withdrew back down the *wadi*. The TOS picquets, having completed their tasks also withdrew back to their HQ, where they were fed before driving back to Izki on 16 November. On the night of 18 November, the TOS set two night ambushes around Izki but there was no rebel activity and 'Gibb Force' returned to Sharjah.

The operation ended as a propaganda victory for the rebels. It did, however, bring out many lessons that were put to good use in later assaults in these mountains.

The War Office department dealing with the matter of regimental colours noted the change of the unit's name and again deferred their decision.

Major R L J Pott MC, King's Own Border Regiment, late of the Sudan Defence Force, joined the TOS and had spent his first month visiting all its locations, including 'Gibb Force' in Oman. He was then appointed Adjutant and was involved in the reorganisation of the TOS for the next nine months. Mulazim Hassan Abdulla Noman remained as Arab Adjutant.

The TOS Intelligence organisation establishment was still one major. Proposals were put forward that this should be increased by one captain to work in HQ and one *mulazim* for the field-force element.

Captain Binns completed his tour and left on 30 November. Captain C M Craigie, Royal Army Medical Corps, replaced him.

Captain Birchall returned from leave and went to the Training Centre.

December

Active patrolling over the whole territory was carried out in response to rumours of movements of arms to the rebels in Oman. B Squadron set up a camp at Al Qair, some eighty miles south-west of Ibri and patrolled to Umm al Zamul. D Squadron set up ambushes around Dhank and the Fatah gap but no contact reports were recorded.

The wrangling between the War Office and the Foreign Office over funding the TOS reached a new climax. The War Office claimed that to carry out their 'strategic' requirements, a force only half the present strength would be needed. Regarding the internal security role, the War Office suggested that the 'Foreign Office should make their own arrangements'. This meant that no more officers were being sent out to replace those whose tours of duty had ended until the matter had been resolved.

At the end of the year the force was deployed as follows:

A Squadron was at Al Khatt.

B Squadron moved to Ibri.

C Squadron was presumably in Sharjah.

D Squadron was still at Jahili.

Training Centre at Manama was under Major Gibb.

World Events 1957

January	Aden	Yemeni incursion into Aden Protectorate repulsed by British forces.
October	Moscow	USSR launched Sputinik I unmanned space satellite.

Notes

1 These weapons were received from the Royal Marines who had taken them to be presented to the Sultan of Oman for his armed forces. It was rumoured that the Sultan asked for a live firing demonstration and was not impressed by the effect of the weapon upon one of the forts and, as he 'did not foresee any threat from tanks at that time', the gift was declined.

2 The higher figure (up from 7*s.* 6*d.*) was authorised as the result of a visit of Major General Bastyn in charge of Administration in Middle East Command, who supported the case for an increase.

3 The arrival of the PR, Sir Bernard and Lady Burrows and myself doubled the European population of Abu Dhabi for a few days. The others were the Political Officer, Mr Martin Buckmaster, Mr and Mrs Tim Hillyard of ADMA and their three-year-old daughter.

10

1958

January

It was decided to move the TOS post at Humar eastwards to Maria and lay out a new airstrip suitable for the Twin Pioneer aircraft now used by the RAF.[1] Captain Burnard and a British signaller with a ground-to-air radio set sent to Humar with the supply camel caravan. Between 10 and 19 January, the Commandant with a small group, including the Signal Officer, accompanied Mr Martin Buckmaster, the Political Officer Abu Dhabi, on his visit to the Liwa. They turned south at Tarif for Bidia where two Bedford trucks followed to dump petrol. At Maria, the party spent one week erecting the new camp. The others arrived from Humar by camel. The post was stocked with petrol and aviation fuel by parachute from a Valetta and the party returned to Sharjah.

One troop of C Squadron was located at Tarif in the old RAF huts. The reduction in the quality of water available there from PDTC prevented the deployment of any more sub-units in the west.

The War Office agreed in a letter dated 13 January to the appointment of a Colonel Commandant for the TOS who would be based in the UK to oversee the selection of British personnel. Sadly, Brigadier Baird, who had been recommended for the post, had died just before and the matter rested.

Shaikh Hazza' bin Sultan al Nahyan, the brother of the Ruler of Abu Dhabi, died on 20 January. He had been his brother's representative in the Liwa and western areas, had attended the Arbitration Tribunal in Geneva in 1955 and had been a good friend to the TOS.

At the end of the month the PR and Lady Burrows visited Abu Dhabi, Buraimi, Ras Al Khaima and Manama, presumably with an escort from the TOS.

February

The Annual Administrative Inspection preparations started.

In Oman, the rebels had re-started mining the tracks around the Jabal Akhdar and the Sultan's Armed Forces, as they were now called, requested the assistance of one squadron of TOS to provide convoy escorts based on Izki.

On the way, with a troop of Ferret scout cars of the 13th/18th Royal Hussars, Major Budd's A Squadron had a Bedford truck mined near Tanuf. The squadron made a new camp site at Izki, their old one being occupied by the NFR. Their task meant that they lost the leading vehicle of almost every convoy blown up by a mine. After some weeks, the PDO oil company refused to use the road through the Wadi Sumail at all so that the only vehicles using the road were SAF supply trucks.

The mines used were small anti-tank mines which did not do fatal damage to vehicles larger than Landrovers except when laid in pairs. 110 vehicles, civilian, PDO, SAF and TOS were mined in this short period of a few months. The American light mines used, which had been supplied to Saudi Arabia, were similar to the British No 75 Hawkins Grenade light anti-tank mine of the 1939–40 period. They weighed under 3 kilogrammes each, so this very disruptive campaign would have needed only five normal 100-kilogramme camel loads to reach the rebels.

March

A reconnaisance team from the British Joint Intelligence Bureau, Middle East, visited the Liwa. It was probably escorted by the TOS and visited the post at Maria.

During the month the TOS were patrolling the Izki and Mutti areas by night to deter rebels from mining the tracks.

On 31 March, Captain Peter Chambers of A Squadron was killed leading a patrol near Mutti and Sergeant Saleh Thani Nayadi and Jundi Saif Said Naimi were wounded. The patrol was ambushed at close range and Captain Chambers shot dead as he charged the enemy who escaped.

April

Two days later, Tactical HQ with additional signallers and the Commandant's bodyguard went by road to Izki via Buraimi and Ibri. They were joined by Major Craig-Adams's B Squadron, who came from Ibri to Izki by the 'outside route', through Fahud to relieve A Squadron. They had two trucks blown up on mines on their approach to Izki. The thorn zariba around the camp was soon replaced by barbed wire, trenches and stone *sangars* with clear fields of fire and the command post was dug in below ground level to meet the increased threat of attack.

Landrover patrols from Izki covered the area from 20 miles east into the Wadi Sumail to fourteen miles westwards on the Fahud track. Their foot patrols covered the tracks about the villages themselves and night ambushes were laid up and down the tracks and at the foot of the Jabal. Some mine detectors had arrived and men of the TOS were trained in their use. During the first six-week period that B Squadron was there, no mines had been laid and the road had been kept open. The aggressive patrolling had improved both the morale and effect of the local tribal guards.

Whilst the TOS were at Izki in strength, the NFR made a sortie up the Wadi Kamah in the hope of drawing Talib's men down into the open following their withdrawal by night. The hope was that the Venoms and Shackletons would then be able to inflict casualties. The withdrawal took longer than planned, surprise was lost and only a few casualties were believed to have been caused by the Shackleton's anti-personnel bombs.

Major Craig-Adams was blown up in his Landrover near Firq but was uninjured.

The further expansion of the force was being discussed with the War Office to increase in Phase 1 the existing strength of:

from British officers 25 to 39
from British other ranks 43 to 119
from Arab officers 12 to 25

and to reduce Arab other ranks 1,186 to 929.

May

Captain D J Cosgrove, the King's Regiment, joined to become the Mortar Officer. As he was a fluent Arabic speaker and there were no three-inch mortars, he was sent to the Training Centre at Manama to translate the Mortar Training Handbook into Arabic aided by Staff Sergeant Smith, King's Royal Rifle Corps.

The TOS was deployed as follows:

Commandant	Colonel Carter
Deputy Commander	Lieut-Col D J C Bannister
Intelligence Officer	Major Chubb
Adjutant	Major Hammick (no Arab Adjutant)
Signal Officer	Captain Shepherd
Quartermaster	Major Atkinson
Medical Officer	Major Craigie
Workshops Officer	Major Shephard
Paymaster	Captain Wood
HQ Squadron	Major Laing
second-in-command	Captain Amin Ezzadine MBE MC (ex-TJFF)
Training Centre, Manama	Major Maynard took over from Major Gibb. Captain Birchall, Training Officer Captain Green, Training Officer Captain Wilson, Demonstration Troop Mulazim Faisal Sultan Qasimi Mulazim Said Makhsin, Signals Mulazim Mohammed Hassan Instructors included: Sergeant Said al Asri Sergeant Obaid Ali Rashid Sergeant Ali Bakhit
A Squadron (Jahili)	Major Budd
B Squadron (Sharjah less one troop at Mirfa)	Major Craig-Adams, Captain Flood
C Squadron (Idhan)	Major Pott (from Captain Foulds on return from leave) Mulazim Hassan Abdullah Noman (from RHQ) Mulazim Faisal Sultan al Qasimi
D Squadron (Ibri)	

Major Gibb left the TOS on 17 May, having completed his tour.

June

The War Office agreed to make the REME Vehicle Inspectorate Team available for annual inspections of the TOS vehicles and technical equipment.

Captain Shepherd returned from mid-tour leave to hand over the signals troop to an officer of the Royal Corps of Signals who had recently arrived and himself took over command of B Squadron in Jahili from Major Craig-Adams, who was going on four months' inter-tour leave. The Squadron second-in-command was Captain F de Vivenot, Royal Artillery; Mulazim Mohamed Saleh and Mulazim Miftah Abdullah were the Arab officers. Their training concentrated on physical fitness with route marches, and weapon training in anticipation of renewal of the operations in Oman in the winter.

C Squadron at Idhan were also training hard in addition to patrolling in the hills.

Captain Birchall left the unit having completed his tour.

July

The revolution in Iraq by General Kasim added more anti-British propaganda to that of Radio Cairo beamed to south-east Arabia. Vehicles were again being mined in Oman, there had been explosions in Muscat itself. British troops were again being flown into Bahrain.

The three-inch mortars first requested in September of 1951 arrived and training with them started under Captain Cosgrove at Manama. The cadre included Corporal Said Suhail bin Noora, Lance Corporals Salim Said Ka'abi and Abdullah Ahmed Balushi. Short-wheelbase Landrovers were modified to carry the mortar detachments and the first two sections were trained.

B Squadron deployed one section to a post in Mahadha and patrolled looking for arms smugglers throughout the area to Hail in the Wadi Jizzi and into Dhank and the Fatah Gap.

August

Captain J C Savage, Royal Artillery, joined.

D Squadron sent a patrol to Buraimi from Ibri taking Shaikh Ali bin Hilal of the Duru and Shaikh Abdullah bin Mohammed al Yaqoobi of Ibri to look for some civilians who had caused a disturbance.

September

Shaikh Said bin Maktoum, the Ruler of Dubai, died on 10 September and was succeeded by his son Shaikh Rashid who had been acting Ruler for some years.

Training at the Jahili was intensified as the weather got cooler, in anticipation of the future operations likely in Oman.

Recruit pay was Rupees 90/= per month (about £6.75). Maximum trade pay was Rupees 300/= (about £22.50).

The blue *mazri* shirt was introduced as part of the TOS dress at about this time.

The TOS were deployed with one squadron less one troop in Sharjah, that troop being at Maria; one squadron less one troop at Ibri, that troop being at Izki; one squadron at Idhan; one squadron less one troop in Jahili, that troop being at Tarif.

The establishment for the enlarged and re-organised Scouts was tabled at meetings in the War Office and for review and approval on 1 April 1959 (see page 180).

October

Captain Shepherd took a troop of B Squadron to climb Jabal Hafit by the southern route, having previously sent Captain de Vivenot with a small reconnaisance party to check the route. Setting out from Jahili, the troop camped at the foot of the Jabal, climbed it with a local guide and breakfasted on the top before returning to the Jahili for lunch.

On 24 October there was a recruits' passing-out parade held at Sharjah for those recruits from Manama who had completed their training. All the Rulers of the Shaikhdoms attended with the exception of the Ruler of Fujairah. Five such parades were planned to take place during each year.

November

B Squadron were relieved by D Squadron from Ibri and returned to Sharjah. Major Craig-Adams re-assumed command of B Squadron on his return from leave and Captain Shepherd became second-in-command. One troop was still at Tarif.

To seal the north-western approaches to the Jabal Akhdar, a squadron was deployed at Yanqul as part of the build-up of the SAF operations in Oman. This must have been D Squadron, who could have returned to be based at Ibri and would have been again under command of Major Steggles, who had rejoined. Captain G A Harford, Royal Artillery, and Captain Vines were the two half-squadron commanders.

The detachment at Yanqul assisted in the arrest of Ghusn bin Saif at the request of the Sultanate Ministry of Interior on a charge of gun-running. The man was tricked into going to Ibri, away from his associates, there he was arrested, brought to Sharjah by road and flown to Muscat.

It was noted in the War Office that the proposed expansion of the TOS had been delayed by some three months and that Phase I would be implemented on 1 January 1959, with Phase II coming into effect on 1 January 1960.

December

The new Political Resident, Sir George Middleton, and his wife were escorted by the Commandant and a small troop of B Squadron in three Landrovers from Khor Fakkan, where they had been landed by the Royal Navy, to Fujairah and to Dubai through the Wadi Qaur.

Just before Christmas, C Squadron from Dhaid, under Major Pott, moved to Awabi and on to Hijar inside the outer ring of mountains to the east of the Jabal Akhdhar at the foot of the central massif.[2] From this base camp they reinforced, with two troops forward, D Squadron of the Special Air Service Regiment, taking over from a company of the NFR on the position nicknamed 'Cassino'. This was some four kilometres west of the 'Aqabat al Dhafar on the plateau at the top of the ancient Persian route up the mountain where the squadron remained for about two weeks. The Life Guards had two Browning machine gun teams with the SAS squadron. C Squadron took over the NFR positions defending the SAS base in a group of stone *sangars* which were roofed with the salvaged khaki and pink supply drop parachutes for protection from the cold and rain.

The Mortar Troop went via the Wadi Jizzi to Rostaq where it camped for one night. The next day, it moved to Awabi where one detachment remained. The other three detachments, using donkeys, went up to Cassino two days later, taking up positions where they fired against rebel mortars in conjunction with the SAS three-inch mortars.

Squadron Sergeant Major Khamis Harib and Sergeants Saif Ahmed bin Maya and Al Asri Said were in C Squadron at that time. Captain Geoff Turner was the squadron second-in-command.

Mulazim Hassan Abdullah Noman was in charge of re-supply from the base camp and Mulazim Faisal Sultan al Qasimi was on leave and not with the squadron on this operation. Lance Corporal Signaller Abdullah Ali Ka'abi was one of the squadron radio operators.

At the end of the year the TOS were deployed as follows:

Commandant	Colonel Carter
Deputy Commander	Lieut-Col Bannister
Intelligence Officer	Captain Woodruff (acting)
Training Centre	Major Maynard
Manama	Captain Wilson
A Squadron (Jahili)	Major Budd
B Squadron (Sharjah, Tarif)	Major Craig-Adams
	Captain Shepherd
	Captain de Vivenot
	Mulazim Mohammed Saleh
C Squadron (Hijar, 'Aqabat al Dhafar)	Major Pott
	Captain Turner
	Mulazim Hassan Abdullah Noman
D Squadron (Ibri, Yanqul)	Major Steggles
	Captain Harford
	Captain Vines
	Mulazim Khalifa Harsoon
Mortar Troop (Hijar, 'Aqabat al Dhafar)	Captain Cosgrove
Independent Troop (Maria)	

World Events 1958

1 February	Cairo	Union of Egypt and Syria proclaimed as the United Arab Republic (UAR)
14 February	Amman	Jordan and Iraq signed an agreement for the union of the two Kingdoms.
21 February	Cairo	Gamal Abdel Nasser became President of the United Arab Republic.
8 March	Sanaa	Yemen federated with the UAR.
May	Aden	State of Emergency declared.
14 July	Baghdad	King Faisal, Crown Prince Abdillah and

		Nuri Said, the Prime Minister, were murdered in a Nasserite army coup led by General Abdel Karim Qassim.
15 July	Lebanon	1,700 US Marines landed in Beirut at the request of the Lebanese government.
17 July	Jordan	2,000 British paratroops landed in Amman at the request of the Jordanian government.
19 July	Cairo	Egypt signed a Defence Pact with the new regime in Iraq.
2 August	Amman	Jordan dissolved the union with Iraq.
October	Lebanon	US troops left Beirut.
November	Jordan	British troops left Amman.
	Paris	General Charles de Gaulle elected as first President of the 5th French Republic.

Notes

1 The Twin Pioneer was a twin-engined, high-wing, fixed-undercarriage slow aircraft with a short take-off and landing capability but it too had small wheels and tyres requiring a firmer surface than that available at Humar. The Anson aircraft, which had landed satisfactorily on the old strips in the Liwa, were no longer in service and the Pembroke communications aircraft, which had replaced them, had such small tyres that they had been unable to use the sandy airstrips of the Liwa.

2 This squadron had earlier been referred to as L Squadron – Light Squadron – for its proposed role in mountain operations but the designation had not stuck.

11

1959

January
In Oman, the Commander of the 22nd Regiment, Special Air Service, Lieut-Colonel Deane-Drummond, arrived on 1 January and, on 12 January, A Squadron of the SAS under Major John Cooper arrived from Malaya. A joint HQ was set up at Nizwa to co-ordinate the operations of the SAS, the Sultan's Armed Forces and the RAF. (The inclusion of the TOS in this joint HQ was not apparent in the records researched.)

C Squadron moved its position eastwards, nearer the 'Aqabat al Dhafar, to better screen the SAS base and to probe for a better route to the north of the 'Aqabat. Earlier shortage of water had been made good by heavy rainfall, which filled pools in the rocks. The TOS positions were in stone *sangars* with parachute cloth over the top as roofs to keep out the rain and as shelter from the sun. A choice of olive drab or pink parachutes was available from those dropped to re-supply the SAS earlier in the operation. Despite the high visability of the pink parachutes, revealing the location of their inhabitants, they had to be used on the headquarters and stores areas as no other tentage was made available.

Two Dhofari soldiers from C Squadron deserted, taking a rifle and a Bren gun, but were caught near Nizwa on their way home to Dhofar.

Between 8 and 22 January, D Squadron of the SAS and A Company of the NFR carried out offensive patrols from Tanuf and drove the rebels from some high ground they were using as an observation post. From 18 to 22 January, A Squadron of the SAS, supported by C Squadron of the TOS and the TOS Mortar Troop, made probing attacks against the 'Aqabat al Dhafra. On the night of 23 January, all but one troop of A Squadron SAS disengaged and went across the mountain to join their D Squadron near Tanuf.

The TOS C Squadron and Mortar Troop continued to engage the rebels on the 'Aqabat to make them believe that the main attack would come at the western end of the Jabal Akhdhar plateau. Also taking part in this deception plan were some 200 Abryeen tribesmen and a platoon of the Muscat Regiment under the command of Major Jasper Coates, who were to climb the two tracks from Awabi to create a further diversion on the north side of the mountain. Both Talib and Ghalib, together with a large number of their men, went to reinforce their positions on the 'Aqabat to more than a 100 strong. They were to be eight hours march away from the real attack when it was launched. Their main strength was concentrated in the west, on the Tanuf track, in response to deliberately planted 'secret' information that the locally recruited donkey men were to be leading their animals up that track from the south on the night of the assault.

At 2030 hours on 26 January, the operation began with a silent climb by the two squadrons of SAS up the mountainside to the east of the Wadi Kamah, not up the *wadi* itself. Only one small rebel outpost of two men with a .50-inch Browning machine gun was found to be guarding that route. The two men were half asleep in their cave and were killed by a single grenade. A Squadron SAS reached its first objective and D Squadron passed through them onto their three objectives further up the mountain.

During that night, C Company of the NFR had relieved A Squadron SAS and the troop of the Life Guards with their dismounted .30-inch Browning machine guns had moved up onto one of the D Squadron SAS positions. Thereafter A Squadron SAS went on to take further objectives on the top of the Jabal and, finally, D Squadron SAS passed through to take up positions beyond them overlooking the village of Habib.

By dawn, after nine and a half hours' climb, the main objectives had all been captured. Habib was then occupied and the three Valetta aircraft from Bahrain made their supply drops of equipment, ammunition, food and water by parachute. The rebels saw the parachutes and believed them to be paratroops, which added to their assessment of defeat. The rebel force melted away and the leaders escaped unobserved down the mountain, later reaching safety in the Sharqiya. During that day, Venoms from Sharjah maintained standing patrols over the area but found no targets. However, their presence had contributed greatly to the final success.

About a week after the capture of the Jabal, D Squadron under

Major Steggles with Captain Wilson as second-in-command, relieved C Squadron. The Mortar Troop, under Captain Cosgrove, remained. WO2 Jimmy Anderson (RAMC) from the TOS Medical Centre was based up on the plateau with the TOS troop in the camp made of pink parachutes. Both sub-units carried out patrols on the plateau for some weeks.

A new base camp had been set up at Hijar by C Squadron, who remained in the area patrolling the lower *wadis*. A troop on patrol under Sergeant Al Asri Said had taken up a position astride a *wadi* leading to a pro-rebel village when about 20 armed men advanced upon them. Sergeant Al Asri kept two sections under cover until the hostile group were entrapped and then he disarmed them without firing a shot.

Some days later, a B Squadron troop, under command of Captain Shepherd and with Mulazim Mohammed Saleh, went to Khor Fakkan on patrol and to co-operate there with the Royal Navy Frigate HMS *Loch Inche*, one of the three ships on patrol in support of the Oman operation.

Talib and Ghalib moved from the Sharqiya where they had hidden and escaped by *dhow* to Saudi Arabia.

Captain Shepherd and Captain Woodruff, the acting Intelligence Officer, were attached to the SAS patrols on the Jabal Akhdhar to act as their interpreters. These patrols lasted two weeks.

The Abu Dhabi Marine Areas oil company at Das Island found commercial quantities of oil.

February

The TOS Mortar Troop left the Jabal and returned to Manama. Radio Cairo had earlier broadcast reports that they had all been killed by the rebels.

A Squadron were at Ibri and had been carrying out patrols in the northern part of the Jabal Akhdhar.

C Squadron left Hijar and returned through the Wadi Jizzi to Jahili. The men cheered when the sands to the west of Buraimi came in sight, glad to be out of the hills and rocks of Oman. There was a plague of locusts in the Dhahira and the Squadron fought the 'hoppers' with poison and, when that ran out, by burning them on the bushes with petrol.

March

B Squadron had moved to Tarif, erected a camp on the western end of the Mirfa feature, and patrolled into the Bainuna.

Captain Shepherd left the TOS at the end of his tour.

The rebel leaders, Talib and Ghalib, arrived in Dammam about 17 or 18 March.

D Squadron moved off the Jabal Akhdhat and out of the Sultanate to camp at Kalba where they stayed for more than four months patrolling the Batinah Coast up to Khor Fakkan. Captain Wilson and Captain Vine were the half-squadron commanders under Major Steggles. Corporal Signaller Abdullah Ali Ka'abi was the squadron radio operator.

The Mortar Troop, now with Mulazim Faisal Sultan al Qasimi as second-in-command, toured squadron locations and carried out demonstrations of the three-inch mortar firing. They visited D Squadron at Kalba, C Squadron at Jahili, A Squadron in Ibri and those at Sharjah, returning to their base at Manama.

The first pipers and drummers started training at Manama.

The Political Agent submitted a report in which he emphasised that the TOS should again be presented as a force serving the Rulers of the Trucial States and not as a unit of the British Army, which it might have been considered locally as a result of its participation in the Jabal Akhdhar campaign in support of the Sultan of Muscat and Oman. He recommended that the force should not be used outside the territory without consultation with the Trucial Council of Rulers.

April

The last TOS squadron to withdraw from Oman was A Squadron, with Major Budd and Captain Stevens, which left Ibri.

An unofficial report of the total of TOS casualties during the Jabal Akhdhar operations states that one British officer was killed, three Arab other ranks were killed and ten Arab other ranks were wounded.[1] This is misleading as only one Arab other rank death in action, at Firq, is known.

Captain W F Stockdale joined the TOS and was posted to C Squadron in Jahili.

On 30 April, Colonel Carter ordered that the TOS flag at the HQ in Sharjah should be flown at half-mast that day in response to the broadcast from Radio Cairo announcing that he had been killed in action by rebel forces in Oman. As this was the third time his death had been claimed by Radio Cairo, it was felt that some recognition was due.

May

About 11 May, fighting broke out between the Abadla tribesmen of Tayyiba, loyal to the Ruler of Fujairah, and the Mazroui tribesmen of 'Asima, followers of the Ruler of Ras al Khaima. A patrol from C Squadron, under Major Pott and Captain Stockdale, went to Fara, collected the *amir* there as guide, and spent most of the night clearing boulders to make a track through the *wadi* up to 'Asima. The next morning they found that the people of Tayyiba had burnt several houses in 'Asima and some goats had been killed. One troop of C Squadron went on to set up a temporary tented post on the Fujairah side of Masafi, under Captain Stockdale. Another patrol, under Captain Vining, was sent to Siggi, and the remainder of the squadron was at Dhaid where Mulazim Hassan Abdullah Noman was responsible for building the new camp.

On 21 May, the Political Agent, with Lieut-Col Bannister Acting Commander TOS and Major Chubb met the Ruler of Ras al Khaima and the Ruler of Fujairah at Manama. Both Rulers agreed to refer the dispute to arbitration and C Squadron remained in the area to keep the peace by patrolling the area Tayyiba, 'Asima, Fara, Ghail, Idhen, Masafi, Habhab and Khatt.

June

About 4 June, C Squadron sent out patrols on hired camels in two columns across the mountains to reach Dibba, where there had been unrest between the Qawasim and the Sharqiin. Major Pott's patrol started from Al Khatt with 30 camels and Captain Stockdale's patrol came over from Masafi with 43 camels. When the two patrols had converged on Dibba they put on a firepower demonstration for the entertainment of the disputing parties. The hiring of the camels had been arranged by sending off individual soldiers to hire them for themselves and their baggage, with a few extra for the officers etc, with payment in cash on return.

D Squadron returned from Kalba to Sharjah at about this time from where they continued anti-smuggling patrols.

July

In Oman, sporadic mining of the roads had started again: the rebels were using modern heavier American and Egyptian anti-tank mines, which could destroy a Landrover and sometimes caused fatal casualties. These incidents provided Radio Cairo with 'evidence' that there was still a full-scale war in Oman.

The TOS, Royal Navy, RAF and the King's Regiment from Bahrain took part in an exercise in the western areas from 22 to 25 July. Part of C Squadron was involved in these exercises and remained at Baraka for about six months. Mulazim Hassan Abdullah Noman with one troop returned to the Liwa to re-establish the post at Maria. They used camels for the deployment and carried out camel patrols mainly in the eastern part of the Liwa.

In the absence of Brigadier Tinker from Bahrain on leave, Colonel Carter visited Muscat between 22 and 28 July as Acting Commander Land Forces Persian Gulf.

Captain Stockdale was at 'Asima on 4 July when the Political Agent visited the area.

August

Captain Amin Ezzadine had been promoted to major.

Captain Cosgrove was appointed Intelligence Officer for the Buraimi Oasis area to be based at the Jahili, where he remained until the completion of his tour in October 1961. Captain D E G Nield, the King's Regiment, became Mortar Officer.

The Deputy Director of Military Intelligence at the War Office had interviewed me at the end of my tour of regimental duty in Germany and agreed to my concept of a network of specially trained 'Desert Intelligence Officers' to operate overtly in the Gulf States. As a result, I was posted to Headquarters Land Forces Persian Gulf (HQLFPG) in early August as the Senior Desert Intelligence Officer (SDIO). Oman was the obvious first target area and my plan was to build upon the local TOS organisation which I had left in 1957.

In the Trucial States and the Sultanate of Muscat and Oman a mixed collection of British military intelligence personnel had accumulated over the period of the Oman revolts, each reporting to his particular parent organisation. There had been an IO in the TOS since early 1956 responsible to the Commandant for gathering, collating and dissemminating military, political and tribal intelligence for the area affecting TOS operations and preparing reports to

LLFPG in Bahrain. Likewise, the Muscat Armed Forces had their own Intelligence Officers serving them but with no obligatory link with Bahrain. During the operations around the Jabal Akhdhar, a certain lack of Intelligence co-ordination became obvious and the available resources of the local authorities for Intelligence gathering were neither fully realised nor used.

The concept of the DIO organisation was that it would provide a framework, initially in Oman and the Trucial States where there was a current threat to security, of 'resident' Intelligence Officers working overtly with local armed forces and with the local Ruler's sources of information. These officers were to have been given a basic training in Intelligence-gathering techniques to ensure a common professional standard. They had dual responsibilities: to the force to which they were attached (TOS or SAF) and to their own organisation, based in HQLFPG in Bahrain. To this end, I had planned to spend a few weeks setting up local contacts in the area of one of the military bases such as Ibri, hand over to the incoming permanent DIO for the area and move to the next-door district, set it up and hand over and so on. In theory, this meant that the SDIO would have personal knowledge of not only the DIOs and their areas but also of their immediate contacts. Having established this network, the SDIO would then be able to comment on authenticity of reports and on any likely bias. In addition, the SDIO would be able to stand in for any DIO in the field if necessary. This was the theory; in practice the DIO destined for Ibri was 'intercepted' by SAF and installed directly in Nizwa.

The prime target was the rebel gun-running and mine-laying activity which required the building up of information about the personal movements of individuals likely to be involved. This meant keeping a card-index system, putting in the information and cross referencing and then retrieving the data, all done in Bahrain. In addition to feeding information back to Bahrain, the DIO had to keep the DIOs on his flanks constantly informed. For example, at its simplest, DIO a and DIO c report the movement of a small caravan and the man x but DIO b has not heard of him. Now alerted, DIO b could investigate further and help to build up a picture of x's movements which might, or might not, coincide with an outbreak of mine-laying incidents.

It did happen, in time. A man's absence from his usual haunts in Inner Oman was reported and correlated with his having been seen in Dammam. As he was a desert guide knowing the routes to Oman from Saudi Arabia through the sands, I arranged that a watch was set on the wells that he would have had to have used should he return that way with contraband. In the event, he came by *dhow* to Dubai but, before the vessel entered the creek, he was warned that patrols were out looking for him, so he disposed of his consignment of mines in the sea and continued his journey harmlessly. He made no secret of his experience when he returned home which may well have dissuaded others from attempting a similar venture, and certainly gave a member of my team in Ibri considerable satisfaction to hear him telling the tale. I believed this to be an effective way to weaken the rebel organisation.

There was no Intelligence cover between the newly appointed IO in Buraimi and Nizwa, the NFR base. My 'Awamir friends knew the Ibri area, the main centre between Buraimi and Nizwa, and were willing and able to work with me there so it seemed a good place to start. Having renewed old contacts in Dubai and the TOS, from whom I borrowed a Landrover, Corporal Signaller Mayouf Awadh and a C12 radio set, I went to Buraimi to meet up with A Squadron and Captain Cosgrove. Whilst there I visited and outlined my task to Shaikh Zayed as I wanted his permission to recruit ex-Sergeant Major Ali Azayz who was by then working for him. This was readily given and so part of the 'old firm' were together again.

Major Budd and a large patrol from A Squadron escorted us to the Sultan's Armed Forces camp at Ibri. For administrative convenience, and to provide an initial cover story, we were to be a TOS liaison team, on their radio net, using my old call sign '17'. Our task was to provide 'flank liaison' with the Muscat Regiment Company at Ibri, commanded by Captain Roger Musker, who replaced the NFR company a few days later.

Captain Savage and Squadron Sergeant Major Humaid Nasr al bu Said were with A Squadron in Jahili.

September

On 16 September, the Political Resident, Sir George Middleton, took the salute at a passing-out parade at Manama and presented the Military Medal to Squadron Sergeant Major Khamis Harib.

A draft Army Council Instruction of the terms of service of British officers and other ranks seconded to the TOS was circulated. It laid down that officers should attend a short language course at the

Command Language School in Aden before joining and that they could qualify for Language Pay at 4*s*. per day at the higher rate for proficiency in both written and spoken Arabic and 2*s*. 6*d*. per day for proficiency in spoken Arabic only.[2] The first tour of duty for which they could volunteer would be for 18 months, with mid-tour and end-of-tour leave. During their tour, they could apply to serve one or more further tours of nine months with similar leave periods. Lieutenant-colonels and above were required to serve for three-year tours.

October

D Squadron, under Major Steggles and Captain Wilson, took part in Exercise Phantom I, which lasted from 8 to 15 October. This was a joint exercise based on Nizwa under control of the SAF, with one company of the King's Regiment from Bahrain, A Squadron of the Life Guards from Sharjah with their Ferret scout cars, and the NFR and one squadron of the TOS. It took place in the general area Jabal Kawr, Ghafat, Bahla, Hamra and Nizwa. D Squadron was deployed to the west and south of Jabal Kawr across the Ibri to Nizwa route for the week-long exercise designed to practise the command and control of all the units and to put troops into back areas that might be refuges for rebel mine-layers.

The British infantry company, commanded by their Company second-in-command, was sent to the head of the *wadi* to the east of Jabal Kawr beyond Ghafat, to make a base camp. From there they were to climb and explore the col joining Jabal Kawr to the hills running down from Jabal Akhdhar. A Royal Engineer survey party were also accompanying the exercise to enable them to carry out their own work in that area.

This particular terrain was relatively unknown to the NFR Intelligence Officer Major Malcolm Dennison and we decided that I should go with the British troops, ostensibly as their interpreter and contact-man with the local village. This suited me as I was trying to discover proof of hidden smuggling routes through the western side of the foothills of the Western Hajar that led to the Balad Sait, Hamra plain and the western routes to the Jabal Akhdhar (see Maps 1 and 6). I was also interested to see whether with the beard I was then growing, my nondescript uniform and the Levantine accent I could mimic would together conceal my British identity from the villagers.

The British troops' first attempt to climb to the col, starting after breakfast, failed as they had to return with a number of potential heatstroke cases. After consultations with me, their patrols set off at dawn the following day, breakfasted on the col, completed their initial tasks and returned safely. This was a sub-unit that had come from Bahrain to gain 'desert experience' and was expected to have had basic knowledge of the dangers of heatstroke.

The RE survey party had air photographs and our study of them showed a track leading into and away from an apparently impassable area of basalt rocks close by our camp. The next day I searched for the track's entrance to the hills and found a small white stone amongst the black basalt beside one of a number of openings wide enough for my Landrover. When the passage became too narrow for the vehicle, we went forward on foot to find steps cleanly cut in the steep places useable by laden camels and donkeys. The route led through onto the plain with Hamra away in the distance. That basalt area could hide an army and was part of the evidence I was looking for.

On 22 October Ali Azayz and I arrived at Jahili having travelled incognito by the part of the suspected smuggling route through the foothills north of Yanqul. It had taken our little party five days by camel from Ibri. The aim was to confirm that the rebels had built up a well organised network of helpers and sympathisers on certain camel routes running northwards along and through the Western Hajar Mountains. Our party consisted of a 'local guide', a camel boy (both relations of Ali Azayz and well known to me), Ali himself and myself. We two acted the part of those 'connected with the rebel operations to the south on their way back to Saudi Arabia' and each carried a .303inch Number 5 rifle, known locally as *barashut* that had been captured from the rebels. As I had always made a point when in Ibri of wearing TOS uniform, it was Captain Musker who took me out of the camp, bearded and suitably disguised, in the back of his Landrover during the afternoon siesta, to the place where the rest of the party, with my camel, would pass at sundown. We made our way northwards as people who did not seek to attract attention. However, we did meet face-to-face with a party of five probably genuine rebels on their way south. We were 'handed on' and guided by rebel helpers through the route from Yanqul to Fatah and behind the hills to Sa'a. This section of the rebel organisation appeared to be working well. The 'phoney rebel party' vanished at Tawi Malagat where my Landrover, which had been driven up from Ibri by Corporal Signaller Mayouf Ahmed, met me with a change of clothes. Freshly shaven and once again the SDIO, I visited the DIO at Jahili, Captain Cosgrove, and returned to Ibri that night. A full report was sent to Bahrain and the relevant information was circulated to DIOs.

A C Squadron detachment completed its work on the airstrip at Dhaid. C Squadron was split between Dhaid and Baraka, possibly as two half-squadrons with Captain Stockdale commanding at Dhaid and Major Pott commanding at Baraka. The troop at Maria under Mulazim Hassan Abdullah having finished its task, rejoined its squadron at Baraka. There still was a limitation on the water supply available from the PDTC in the west, restricting to numbers of the TOS that could be deployed there.

November

On 12 November, a mine exploded between Buraimi and Al Ain and another exploded near Hamasa on 27 November. Both incidents were in Sultanate territory.

Exercise Phantom II took place. It was a deployment exercise bringing the new Mobile Regiment HQ under Lieut-Col Bannister, D Squadron again, a section of the Mortar Troop and A Squadron of the Royal Dragoons scout cars (who had relieved the Life Guards), into the area between Ibri and Yanqul. In addition, a strong camel patrol of the TOS, commanded by a *mulazim*, came from Jahili to Yanqul along the smugglers' route. The Sultan of Oman's Air Force (SOAF) provided an Air Liaison Officer (ALO) to bring in their Pioneer and Provost aircraft for reconnaisance and support.

The TOS HQ group convoy was passing Ma'azam when the Medical Officer's Landrover detonated a large mine under a rear wheel. The MO, his orderly and the driver were thrown up through the canvas roof and landed some distance away, shocked and bruised but otherwise unhurt. The complete rear half of the Landrover had been destroyed and the stores and baggage that had been in it blown to pieces.

D Squadron camped close to Yanqul to patrol the area. The Royal Dragoons were in an unused part of the NFR camp at Ibri, patrolling up the *wadis* and out on the desert fringe to gain experience. The exercise ended some days later with a firepower demonstration staged by Major Steggles and attended by the Wali from Ibri, who brought Shaikh Saif bin 'Amir, many minor Shaikhs and tribesmen from the Yanqul area.

The demonstration opened with one rifleman engaging a petrol-tin target at about 400 yards with ten rounds, Lance Corporal Mohammed Azayz 'Amiri hit with every shot. Next the rifle group in his section engaged other targets and were joined by the Bren group. The whole troop then opened fire including their two-inch mortar. They were joined by the .30-inch Browning machine guns of the Ferret scout cars. The three-inch mortar section added its high explosive and smoke bombs and, finally, two rocket-firing Provost aircraft of the SOAF attacked the targets near the top of the hill in front of the spectators.

Captain de Vivenot left the TOS on completion of his tour.

December

A camel patrol from C Squadron, commanded by Captain Stockdale, spent two weeks in the hills to the south of Masafi. Their base was still in Dhaid at the end of the month.

Major S A R Cawston, Royal Artillery, was Brigade Major and Major G A Charrington, 17th/21st Lancers, was the DAA and QMG.

The War Office were still unwilling to purchase Dodge Power-Wagon vehicles for desert trials by the TOS despite repeated requests and papers written to justify the requirement.

In Dubai, work had started on the airport and development of the port had continued. Plans for the installation of an electricity supply and a telephone system were in hand for completion in 1961 and 1960 respectively.

World Events 1959

January	Cuba	Fidel Castro overthrew the Batista government.
February	Cyprus	EOKA revolt ended with signing of agreement to form a Republic.
November	Kenya	Mau-Mau revolt ended.

Notes

1 Mentioned in Captain Shepherd's book, *Arabian Adventure*, published by Collins in 1961. But I have not been able to find anyone who has heard of these two additional deaths in my interrogation of Arab TOS who took part in the operations.

2 Unchanged since 1953.

12

1960

January

In Ibri, D Squadron 22nd SAS Regiment arrived for about three months' training in desert operations. Their Austin K9 trucks 1-ton 4 x 4 GS cargo and other transport were landed at Sharjah and escorted to Ibri by the TOS Workshops Officer, Captain Bidwell.

On 21 January, acting on information resulting from a penetration of the rebel organisation by my team, the NFR company from Ibri intercepted near Dann (to the north of the Jabal Kaur) a caravan of five camels, carrying a consignment of heavy and light American-made mines. This caravan had crossed the open plain to the east of Ibri, having avoided the SAS motor patrols searching there, and taken cover in a large area of basalt rocks from which they emerged where the NFR Company HQ were resting. Of the three rebels on their way to Jabal Akhdhar, one escaped, one was killed and one captured. Their two camel men had brought them from Miskin in the Wadi Kabir to where they had come after landing from a *dhow* at Saham on the Batina. This route was on another well established chain of rebel sympathisers.

Mulazim Hassan Abdullah Noman left the TOS, having completed eight years' service.

February

Captain P Robertson, DIO attached to the TOS, had arrived and I took him to Masafi where he was to operate, based on the TOS camp there.

March

The TOS Tactical HQ went to the Batina to take part in Exercise Phantom V with the Sultan's Armed Forces (SAF), A Squadron of the Royal Dragoons with their scout cars from Sharjah, D Squadron

SAS from Ibri, and the aircraft carrier HMS *Bulwark* off the Batina Coast. The exercise ended about 11 March.

Plans were put forward for new buildings to be erected on the higher ground outside and to the north-east of the RAF compound for the British Officers' Mess, the British Sergeants' Mess, the Medical Centre and a house for the Commandant.

C Squadron at Mirfa, under command of Major Pott, sent a patrol to the eastern end of the Liwa supported by Bedford trucks.

D Squadron, under Major Steggles, was in Jahili with Captain Stockdale, as his temporary second-in-command, and Captain Griffiths. DIO Buraimi was Captain Cosgrove.

A Ferret scout car of the Royal Dragoons was mined in the western exit from the Wadi Jizzi after the squadron had bivouaced at its eastern approach for the previous night. Despite this lack of security, their newly arrived squadron commander blamed the TOS for failing to prevent the incident, which had taken place in Sultanate territory. The relationship between the TOS and the succession of armoured car squadrons based in Sharjah, dating back to Operation Boxer, depended entirely on the professional experience and personality of their squadron commanders. There were many ups and downs of which this incident was an unfortunate example.

April

A War Office Intelligence report gave the following details of the TOS:

Strength

34 British officers
90 British other ranks
8 Arab officers
1,021 Arab other ranks
50 Boys

Deployment

Force HQ at Sharjah
Training centre at Manama
Five squadrons at Dhaid, Mirfa, Buraimi (Jahili), Khatt and in Sharjah (A, B, C, D, and E Squadrons).
A sixth squadron (X Squadron) was to be formed during 1960 when the Force would be re-organised into a Mobile/

Desert and a Patrol/Internal Security Regiment, each of three squadrons.

An Air Ministry Works Department vehicle from RAF Sharjah was blown up on a mine in the Buraimi area on 8 April.

Most of the SAS personnel had left Ibri by air at the end of their training. One of their Bedfords had been mined near Ma'azam on 4 April so the remainder of their vehicles followed me on a safe route to the west, arriving at Jahili in the afternoon of 20 April. From Jahili they returned to Sharjah.

In the Shaikhdom of Abu Dhabi, a police force had been formed under a British police officer, Mr Stokes. The force was about 160 strong with posts in Al Ain and Abu Dhabi.

May

D Squadron, under Captain Stockdale, moved from Jahili to Mirfa to relieve C Squadron, who were under the temporary command of Captain Vining, Major Pott being on leave.

On 10 May, the Political Resident in Bahrain, through his Military Defence Committee, issued a Directive to the Commander TOS which laid down his tasks as follows:

(1) to prevent or repel any armed incursion into or attack on the Trucial States
(2) to obtain political, military, security, topographical and all manner of intelligence on the Trucial States and the Sultanate of Muscat and Oman
(3) to prevent or suppress any traffic in slaves or illegal traffic in arms
(4) to provide an escort for British political representatives travelling in the Trucial States
(5) to prevent and detect offences committed by any persons in the parts of the Trucial States in which the Force is authorised to operate
(6) to maintain a prison for persons subject to Her Majesty's jurisdiction
(7) to co-operate and maintain liaison with units of the Royal Navy, the British Army and the Royal Air Force operating in the area
(8) to assist the civil power in disasters

In Sharjah, on 25 May, A Squadron Signaller 745 Silaih Salih, of Adeni origin, shot dead 223 Corporal Driver Rashid Ali of Mu'ataradh in the squadron lines. The matter of jurisdiction in this case was the subject of lengthy discussion between the British authorities and the Shaikhs of Abu Dhabi. Major Chubb was president of the Board of Inquiry into the matter, Captain J. Landau as Adjutant, and Captain J T Anderson as Medical Officer and Sergeant Khalifa Hamed of A Squadron gave evidence. Eventually, the accused was found unfit to stand trial due to insanity and deported to a mental institution in Aden. It was later learnt that Driver Rashid Ali was related to a man said to have been involved in the death of a relative of the Signaller and that this murder was in furtherance of this blood feud.

A Squadron under Captain B R C Smith relieved B Squadron at Dhaid.

July

Mulazim Awal Said Mahsin started his signals course at the School of Infantry, Warminster, in the UK on 12 July.

Mulazim Thoma Atallah Adwani, on Temporary Loan from the Arab Legion since 1 January 1951, renewed his terms of service.

A proposal that selected and trained Arab officers of the TOS were to be appointed to Trucial States Commissions, which would have equal status with British officers of the same rank, in addition to the existing Kaid's Commissions, which would retain their intermediate status between warrant officer and commissioned-officer rank was circulating between the Foreign Office and the War Office.

August

Captain Stockdale handed over command of D Squadron to Captain Wallerstein and took over temporary command of C Squadron at Jahili whilst Major Pott was attending the Arabic Language Course in Aden.

No replacement officer was available to take Major Chubb's duties as Intelligence Officer when his tour ended so Major Budd was transferred from command of A Squadron to take up the appointment which he held until December 1971.

About 16 August, Captain G A L Hoad, Royal Artillery, took over the DIO post at Ibri from me. I had been selected to attend the Technical Staff Course at the Royal Military College of Science.

The title of SDIO lapsed and the local DIO organisation became absorbed into the TOS.[1] In time, the resident DIOs of the TOS became channels for the initiation of many civilian projects to the benefit of their areas of responsibility, such as *falaj* repairs and road-making in the hills, which strengthened their individual personal involvement with the inhabitants.

Captain Stockdale, with a troop from C Squadron and a gang of local labourers, built the first road from Masafi down the Wadi Ham through Bithna to the Batina coast. The sum of Rs 1,000 (£75) had been provided by the British authorities in Bahrain to pay for this work and the task was made a little easier by the use of plastic explosive and 'Beehive' demolition charges from British Army sources. Captain Stockdale and the troop returned during the month to Jahili.

Lieut-Col A C Mason and Captain J Savage were noted as being in Force HQ.

Colonel Carter was married in UK and later brought his wife to live in the house next to the Officers' Mess on the Sharjah creekside. This house became known as Flagstaff House and was a fine example of the best of local domestic architecture.

In the course of a road-checkpoint training exercise by the Recruit Training Squad from Manama on the track up to Idhan on 24 August, the Ruler of Fujairah and his party were searched, apparently with the Shaikh's acceptance of the British officer's explanation. The incident was reported by the Ruler to the Political Agent and apologies demanded and given.

September

In a memorandum dated 5 September to Bahrain, the Political Agent, Mr Donald Hawley, set out his views on the current position and future possibilities of the TOS with regard to the Directive issued in May. He expressed concern about the high proportion of British personnel in the force, which was about one in ten. He stressed the need to limit British participation to training and education, in preference to administrative tasks, which the Arab personnel ought now to be able to perform. In this connection, he pressed for the introduction of Arabic words of command and the development of the TOS Boys School as the source of future trained and educated manpower for the force.[2] He also pointed out the lack of an organised security force to cover the towns of Sharjah, Ajaman, Umm al

Quwain, Ras al Khaima, Fujairah, Khor Fakkan, Kalba and the *bedu* areas.

This memorandum looked ahead to the needs of a possibly independent Trucial States federation of some kind and put forward the view, which had been discussed with Colonel Carter, that the TOS should be the principal force for the defence of the Trucial States and as such should be seen to be the Rulers' force. The TOS should also be responsible for a Gendarmerie Force that would be differently trained in a police role and either absorb or co-operate closely with the existing Dubai Police and Abu Dhabi Police Forces. The formation of a Desert Regiment with the capability of operating outside the Trucial States, most likely in Oman, was thought to be of much less importance than the gendarmerie requirement.

The Dubai Police consisted of one British Superintendent, Mr Peter Lorimer, and 90 constables operating in and around the town of Dubai. The Abu Dhabi Police had one British Superintendent and 255 men stationed in both Abu Dhabi and Al Ain.

Mulazims Faisal Sultan Qasimi and Mohammed Saleh went to England and started their six-week course at the Mons Officer Cadet School in Aldershot on 8 September.

Earlier proposals to re-equip the Scouts with the new 7.62mm FN semi-automatic rifles were shelved but their request for six .50-inch Browning medium machine guns was accepted with issues to be made after 1 April 1961. The .303-inch calibre weapons were therefore to be retained for the time being.

The re-deployment planned for 1 October, to base the Desert Regiment HQ and two squadrons in the Buraimi Oasis with one of the squadrons perhaps located in Sultanate territory, was postponed until after the expected visit to the area of a United Nation Commission under a Mr de Ribbing. No 'undue military activity' that might be construed as reinforcements was to take place.

October

New accommodation in Sharjah was planned with Phase I for the British Officers' and British Sergeants' Messes and the Medical Centre with work to begin in October 1961 for completion in 1963–4. Phase II, building new Arab accommodation, was to start at the end of 1962.

C Squadron returned to Sharjah.

On 21 October, a TOS Landrover was stolen by a Dhofari soldier from the recently formed X Squadron. He had taken it into the Sultanate through the Aswad border post and sold it in Muscat or Matrah and absconded. Captain Wilson, commanding X Squadron, took a patrol to reclaim the vehicle but was prevented from so doing by the Sharia Court in Muscat. It appeared that no evidence from Christians, Muslim soldiers and Muslim government officials was acceptable to the Court and the vehicle remained the property of the purchaser.

The decision to recruit men for X Squadron from Dhofar, in the southern part of the Sultanate of Oman, was based partly on the idea that as 'mountain men' and subjects of the Sultan, albeit serving as mercenaries in the Desert Regiment, they would have a useful role in any future 'external' operations in Oman or the Jabal Akhdhar. They turned out to be tough soldiers and eager to learn the military skills on offer. What was not foreseen was the growing Communist influence of the Popular Front for the Liberation of Oman and the Arab Gulf (PFLOAG) in Southern Arabia and its infiltration of the Dhofaris.

Colonel H J Bartholomew OBE, late the King's Own Border Regiment, was selected to succeed Colonel Carter as Commandant.

November

It was decided in London, in a letter dated 8 November, to improve the airstrip at Buraimi to 'Beverley standards' for use by the large RAF tactical transport aircraft that had been used successfully in the Oman campaigns. The airstrip to the east of Al Ain on the gravel plain had been in use from the beginning by Anson, Dakota and Valetta and even a Saudi Airlines Bristol Freighter. These aircraft, with their large tyres on two-wheel undercarriages with tailwheels, had been able to use it without permanent damage to the surface. Later Pembroke and Twin Pioneer aircraft had small twin tyres that cut up the gravel surface and limited its use.

December

In correspondence between Bahrain and London, reference was again made to the Desert Regiment being stationed at Idhan, instead of Buraimi, to avoid complications over the use of Sultanate territory there and the impending visit of the UN Mission.

Near Hamasa, the Sultan of Oman's Air Force had established a short airstrip to accept their Single Pioneer communication aircraft.

A proposal to develop this airstrip to take their Piston Provost armed aircraft and to store a supply of their bombs and rockets there with aviation fuel was not supported by the British authorities, again in view of the expected likely UN Mission visit.[3]

Major E H Hillyard was recorded as being the TOS Medical Officer. Major Langdale, REME, was commanding the TOS Workshops.

Mulazim Faisal Sultan al Qasimi and Sergeant Obaid Ali Rashid were now with X Squadron.

On 27 December, a message from the War Office finally announced that one Dodge Power-Wagon vehicle would arrive in Sharjah for the TOS to test 'within a week or two'.

Provision was made in the financial estimates for 1961–2 for the supply of 24 radio stations BCC HF 156 Mk2 and, on 30 December, the estimated forecast cost of the TOS for the financial year 1961–2 was £1,123,400 shared equally between the Foreign Office and the War Office.

World Events 1960

January	Egypt	President Nasser laid the foundation stone of the new Aswan High Dam to be built with funds from the USSR as the UK/USA funding was withdrawn at the time of Suez Canal nationalisation.
June	Kinshasha	Belgian Congo granted independence.
July	Mogadishu	Former Italian Somaliland united with Somaliland to form the Republic of Somalia.
July	Paris	French Congo (Brazzaville), Chad and the Central African Republic achieved their independence from France.
July	Kinshasha	Katanga province under Moise Tshombe broke away starting the civil war in the Congo.
August	Malaya	State of Emergency lifted.
October	Lagos	Nigeria granted independence.
November	USA	John F Kennedy elected President.

Notes

1 See item (2) of the PR's Directive in May 1960 (page 142).
2 See report of January 1954 (page 47).
3 The UN Mission never did reach the Trucial States.

Conclusion

The 10 years' development of the 'small body of armed police' costing £35,500 in 1951 to the 1,550 strong regiment planned for the 1960s at a cost of £1,123,400 was a remarkable achievement by the four Commandants during this period. They served two masters, the Foreign Office and the War Office, who rarely held the same view of the force and its tasks. They faced a continuous shortage of equipment and personnel to deal with the unusual problems, both political and military, that arose.

The cyclic change in the relationship between the military and the local requirement is perhaps best illustrated by the actual introduction of Arabic words of command in 1954, and again the recommendation that they be used as quoted in the Political Agent's memorandum of 5 September 1960. The pattern of bringing in the mercenary in considerable numbers, Adeni and Dhofari, because of doubts about the numbers or quality of the local manpower, appears in both 1953 and again in 1959. In practice, however, the quality of the local recruits, when properly trained and led, was equal to or better than that of the 'outsiders'.

Improvements in air and radio communications and the eventual arrival of suitable tyres for the unit's vehicles gave the force almost total mobility and control over the desert areas. The need for operations in the mountains and hills meant an emphasis on basic fitness and infantry tactics that had perhaps lapsed during the static post and motor-patrol period of operations. This change from 'survival soldiering', in small isolated outposts that was not far removed from the *bedu* way of life to a more formal military, westernised routine may have taken away some of the romantic aspects of the 'desert warrior' with long hair, featured in early press reports of the activities of the Trucial Oman Levies. These same soldiers showed later that they were capable of holding their own in the Jabal Akhdhar operations and be as smart as any on parade, together with their pipers and drummers.

In the Trucial States over this decade, there had been changes too. The transistor radio had arrived and with it a much wider public knowledge of the world outside. In the early years there were still *bedu* families who had not seen a European or American; electric light was supplied by private generators in a few houses in Dubai and Sharjah apart from the RAF Station; the camel was still the principal means of transport and everyone carried a rifle. By the end of this decade, though there were no tarmac roads yet, the truck had replaced the camel on all routes except that to the Liwa, motorised *'abras* were on the creek in Dubai and it was unusual to see an armed man. The feeling of security that this brought with it on the Trucial Coast created the conditions for a great increase in commercial activity, mainly in Dubai, in advance of the coming of oil.

Externally, the threat of destabilisation of the rest of the Arabian Peninsula by Communist influences had already begun. The winds of change were blowing in the Arab world and the next decade promised to be both dangerous and challenging with great changes brought about by the long-awaited wealth to the Trucial States from oil. The Political Agent's Memorandum of 5 September 1960 did indeed look forward to the needs of 'a possibly independent Trucial States federation of some kind'.

Appendices

1

Roll of Honour

Buraimi November 1953

Major H O D Thwaites MC, 9th Lancers
Flying Officer A L C Duncan, RAF
WO I Daud Sidqi, Arab Legion

Khatwa October 1954

Jundi Khalais al Nayadi, TOL 666

Hamasa October 1955

Jundi Obaid Mubarak al Katabi, TOL
Jundi Sayid al Hadhrami, TOL

Firq August 1957

Jundi Saif Obaidil, TOS 1325

Mutti March 1958

Captain P Chambers MC, Royal Hampshire Regiment

2

Honours and Awards

Honours List
June 1955

OBE	Lieutenant-Colonel W J Martin	

The London Gazette
25 May 1956

OBE	Lieutenant-Colonel E F Johnson MBE, MC	(See page 156)
MC	Captain A R Steggles	(See page 157)
MM	Sergeant Mohammed Nakhaira 143	(See page 158)
MM	Sergeant Nakhaira Mohammed 203	(See page 159)
MM	Lance Corporal Said Salem 107	(See page 160)

Honours List
June 1957

MBE	Major P H Clayton	
BEM	Staff Sergeant H Playfor	

Honours List
June 1958

BEM	Staff Sergeant Said Mahsin	

The London Gazette
21 August 1959

MM	Sergeant Khamis Harib 669	(See page 161)

Mention in Dispatches

	Captain R L G Weir	

Honours List

June 1960

OBE	Colonel S L A Carter MBE, MC
MBE	Major R L J Pott MC

Citations

1 Citations for Honours List awards are not released.

2 Citations for awards published in *The London Gazette* are quoted in the following pages.

3

From *The London Gazette* of Friday 25 May 1956

'In recognition of distinguished service in the Trucial Oman.' Lieutenant-Colonel E F Johnson's appointment to be an Additional Officer of the Military Division of the Most Excellent Order of the British Empire (OBE) was a Gallantry Award for which the following extract from the citation is available:
Place: Trucial States
Date of action or period covered by the citation: 6 November 1954 to date (26 October 1955)
How employed: Commandant, Trucial Oman Levies
Other Detail:
This officer was selected to command the Trucial Oman Levies at a time when the Political Situation in the Persian Gulf was causing grave concern and uneasiness.

During the period of his Command he has displayed initiative, drive, leadership and resource of a high order. He has a sound knowledge of his professional duties and has carried out his duties in an exemplary manner.

Much of his work is of a political nature and outside the scope of an officer's normal duties; it demands close and friendly liaison with the political authorities and Arab leaders and an understanding of Arab politics.

During the Buraimi operation he displayed gallantry, leadership and resource that were an example to all.

The success of the operation was mainly due to his careful planning and to the spirit with which he commanded the Force engaged.

4

From *The London Gazette* of Friday 25 May 1956

'In recognition of gallant and distinguished services in the Trucial Oman.'

Captain A R Steggles's Immediate Award (operational) of the Military Cross (MC) has the following citation:

Place: Hamasa, Buraimi Oasis, Trucial States

Date of action: 26 October 1955

How employed: as a Squadron Commander, Trucial Oman Levies

Other Detail:

This officer led the Squadron in the attack on Hamasa on 26 October 1955. Throughout the initial heavy fighting which lasted from 0530 hours until midday without ceasing, and thereafter at intervals throughout the remainder of the day he displayed at all times coolness of mind; steadiness of action and a high standard of personal courage.

By his bearing and leadership he rallied his troops after their first casualties, drawing from them their utmost efforts throughout the battle.

He dragged one of his wounded men lying in the open through close rifle fire of about two minutes' duration to safety; with no regard for his own personal safety.

On two occasions he approached to within short range of one of the strongly manned Forts of the enemy to use the two-inch mortar against it, on both occasions putting himself completely exposed to the fire of the enemy.

His courage under fire and his command and leadership of his Arab Warrant Officer, Non Commissioned Officers and men in their first major operation was an important factor in the final success of the Buraimi Operation.

5

From *The London Gazette* of Friday 25 May 1956

'In recognition of gallant and distinguished services in the Trucial Oman.'

Sergeant Mohammed Nakhaira's Immediate Award (operational) of the Military Medal (MM) has the following citation:
Place: Hamasa, Buraimi Oasis, Trucial States
Date of action: 26 October 1955
How employed: Troop Sergeant
Other detail:
He was a Troop Sergeant in the initial Squadron attack on Hamasa on 26 October 1955. During the most intense action of the battle his Troop was cut off from its British Squadron Commander and the remainder of the Squadron.

At all times he controlled his men courageously, supporting the remainder of the Squadron in their attacks on forts held by the enemy by well planned and well controlled supporting fire.

In this, his first action under fire, he set a high example to his men of courage, cool nerve and leadership.

6

From *The London Gazette* of Friday 25 May 1956

'In recognition of gallant and distinguished services in the Trucial Oman.'

Sergeant Nakhaira Mohammed's Immediate Award (operational) of the Military Medal (MM) has the following citation:
Place: Hamasa, Buraimi Oasis, Trucial States
Date of action: 26 October 1955
How employed: Troop Sergeant
Other detail:
This NCO was a Troop Sergeant in the Squadron carrying out the initial attack on Hamasa on 26 October 1955. At all times during the most intense fighting he displayed a high standard of leadership. Without regard for his own safety he continually moved about his men exposed to enemy fire, rallying them and controlling their fire.

In this, his first action under fire, he set a high standard and example to his men of courage and cool leadership.

7

From *The London Gazette* of Friday 25 May 1956

'In recognition of gallant and distinguished services in the Trucial Oman.'

Lance Corporal Said Salem's Immediate Award (operational) of the Military Medal (MM) has the following citation:
Place: Hamasa, Buraimi Oasis, Trucial States
Date of action: 26 October 1955
How employed: M.T. NCO
Other detail:
This Non-Commissioned-Officer, in the heat of the fighting for Hamasa on 26th October 1955, took over and drove a Squadron supply truck with reserve ammunition across 200 yards of open ground under heavy fire to the Squadron Headquarters in the village, in the course of which the vehicle was hit twice and he was wounded.

Later, at a time when the Squadron supply route had been cut by an enemy post, he drove a Landrover with a seriously wounded soldier and an urgent dispatch under intense close range enemy fire, to Regimental Tactical Headquarters. He showed no regard for his own personal safety.

He not only carried his duties as Non-Commissioned Officer i/c Transport but was always to be found in the forefront of the battle giving assistance to his Squadron Commander, to the Section leaders and encouragement to young inexperienced soldiers. He displayed the highest standard of personal courage and devotion to duty.

8

From *The London Gazette* of Friday 21st August 1956

'In recognition of gallant and distinguished services in the Arabian Peninsula.'

Military Medal

669 Sergeant Khamis Hareb, Trucial Oman Scouts

For his fine leadership and courage throughout the operations in the Jabal Akhdar. On one occasion he successfully established a troop position undetected by the enemy and thereby greatly facilitated the attack on the 'Aqbat al Dhafar.

9

Commanding Officers of the TOL and TOS and British Commanders of the Union Defence Force

1 Major J M Hankin-Turvin (Arab Legion on FO contract)
January 1951 to August 1953

2 Lieutenant-Colonel W J Martin OBE (Suffolk Regiment)
August 1953 to November 1954

3 Lieutenant-Colonel E F Johnson OBE MC (South Lancashire Regiment)
November 1954 to May 1957

4 Colonel S L A Carter OBE MC (Sherwood Foresters)
May 1957 to March 1961

5 Colonel H J Bartholomew OBE (King's Own Border Regiment)
March 1961 to March 1964

6 Colonel F M de Butts CMG OBE (Somerset and Cornwall Light Infantry)
March 1964 to February 1967

7 Colonel K P G Ive OBE (17th/21st Lancers)
February 1967 to May 1970

8 Colonel H R C Watson MBE (Queen's Regiment)
May 1970 to December 1971
Commander Union Defence Force
December 1971 to March 1974

9 Colonel K Wilson MBE (Royal Scots)
Commander Union Defence Force
March 1974 to 1975

10

British Political Representatives in Bahrain and the Trucial States 1950 to 1971

Political Residents Persian Gulf in Bahrain

1951	Sir Rupert Hay
1957	Sir Bernard Burrows
1960	Sir George Middleton
1961–6	Sir William Luce
1966 71	Sir Stewart Crawford
1971	Sir Geoffrey Arthur

Political Agents Trucial Coast in Sharjah

1948–51	P D Stobart
1951	A J Wilton
1952	M S Weir (M Buckmaster temporarily attached)

Political Agents Trucial Coast in Dubai

1953	M S Weir
1954–5	C M Pirie-Gordon (J Walker temporarily attached)
1955–8	J P Tripp
1958–61	D F Hawley
1961–4	A J M Craig
1964–6	H M Balfour-Paul
1966–8	D A Roberts
1968–71	J L Bullard

Political Officers in Abu Dhabi

1956–8	Hon M Buckmaster
1958–9	E R Worsnop
1959–61	E F Henderson

Political Agents in Abu Dhabi

1961–5	Colonel Sir Hugh Boustead
1965–8	A T Lamb
1968–71	C J Treadwell

Ambassador to the United Arab Emirates

1971	C J Treadwell

11

Pay Scales for the Trucial Oman Levies, January 1951

Basic pay		Rs 60/= per month*
plus dearness allowance of ⅓		Rs 20/= †
Private Soldier (Jundi) total		Rs 80/= per month
Lance Corporal (Jundi Awal) plus		Rs 10/=
Corporal (Areef)		Rs 15/=
Sergeant (Naib)		Rs 25/=
Warrant Officer (Wakil)	from	Rs 50/=
	to	Rs 100/=
Arab officers – 2nd Lieutenant (Mulazim Thani) rising by Rs 10/= per month per year		Rs 200/=
Stoppages for all ranks		Rs 5/=
Trade Pay		
Driver 1st class		Rs 30/=
Driver 2nd class		Rs 20/=
Driver 3rd class		Rs 10/=
Signaller 1st class		Rs 30/=
Signaller 2nd class		Rs 20/=
Signaller 3rd class		Rs 10/=
Medical orderly 1st class		Rs 30/=
Medical orderly 2nd class		Rs 20/=
Medical orderly 3rd class		Rs 10/=

There was an additional rate of trade pay for drivers and mechanics of Rupees 50/= to 60/= during the first six months to equate to the civilian drivers etc initially recruited.

*One Indian Rupee was worth 1*s.* 6*d.*
†The 'dearness allowance' was a means of increasing the total pay by one-third to bring it closer to oil-company-labourer rates.

12

Revised Establishment of March 1953 and Planned Organisation

The new TOL establishment was agreed as follows:

Personnel

5 x British officers (Commander, Second-in-Command/Adjutant Quartermaster/Administrative, 2 x Training Officers)
6 x British NCOs (technical and specialist duties)
10 x Arab Officers* (Assistant Adjutant, Training and Company Commanders)
2 x Arab Warrant Officers Class 1 (RSM, RQMS)
5 x Arab Warrant Officers Class 2 (CSMs, Accounts)
22 x Arab Sergeants (including specialists)
41 x Arab Corporals (including specialists)
Rank and File:
7 x Fitters
6 x Clerks
7 x Storemen
24 x Signallers
1 x Armourer
5 x Runners
63 x Drivers
15 x Cooks
276 x Riflemen
Total 511

*These Arab Officers were expected to come from Aden but suitable personnel could not be found. A further 6 British Officers were therefore agreed and are shown as such in the outline re-organisation shown below.

Vehicles

14 x trucks ¼ ton GS Landrover
36 x trucks 1 ton GS cargo
8 x trucks 3 ton GS cargo
4 x trucks 1 ton GS water
1 x truck 3 ton GS recovery
1 x truck 3 ton GS machinery
14 x trailers ½ ton light weight
8 x trailers 1 ton cargo

Weapons

22 x pistols .38-inch revolver
414 x rifles .303-inch No 4 with bayonets
36 x sub-machine guns 9mm STEN
39 x light machine guns .303-inch BREN
12 x mortars 2-inch OML
12 x Wireless sets No 19

The intended expanded organisation in outline was:

Regimental HQ	Commanding Officer Second-in-Command Adjutant Medical Officer Quartermaster Senior Arab Officer Arab Regimental Sergeant Major (RSM) Arab Regimental Quartermaster Sergeant (RQMS)
Headquarter Squadron	Commander Arab Officer Non-Commissioned Officer
Signal Troop	Regimental Signals Officer Arab NCOs and Signallers
Motor Transport Troop	Motor Transport Officer NCO Arab Drivers and Mechanics
Administrative Troop	Arab Clerks, Cooks, Cleaners etc

Three Line Squadrons
each:

Squadron HQ	Commander
	Arab Officer
	Non-Commissioned Officer*

Three troops under command of a Senior Arab NCO made up of three sections of ten men under an Arab Junior NCO

*British NCOs were not available in the numbers required and did not serve with line squadrons. Arab Squadron Sergeant Majors and Squadron Quarter Master Sergeants were found instead.

13

Rates of Additional Pay for British Ranks seconded to the TOL

The additional daily rates of pay were agreed in May 1953:

Local Overseas Allowance

Lieutenant-Colonel	2/7d	(two shillings and sevenpence)
Other officers	2/3d	(two shillings and threepence)
Warrant Officer I	2/9d	(two shillings and ninepence)
Warrant Officer II and Staff Sergeant	2/7d	(two shillings and sevenpence)
Sergeant	2/5d	(two shillings and fivepence)
Corporal	2/3d	(two shillings and threepence)

Additional Class C (Inducement Pay) Allowance

Lieutenant-Colonel	11/=	(eleven shillings)
Major	8/6d	(eight shillings and sixpence)
Captain	6/=	(six shillings)
Lieutenants	4/6d	(four shillings and sixpence)
Warrant Officers	3/6d	(three shillings and sixpence)
Staff Sergeants and below	3/=	(three shillings)

Ration Allowance (payable when away from Sharjah)

All ranks	7/6d	(seven shillings and sixpence)

Language Qualification Pay (awarded after examination)

Colloquial	2/=	(two shillings)
Interpreter	4/=	(four shillings)

14

Official Statement on the Buraimi Oasis Dispute by the Foreign Office 5 October 1955

By the agreement of July 30, 1954, between the Government of the United Kingdom (acting on behalf of the Ruler of Abu Dhabi and the Sultan of Muscat) and the Government of Saudi Arabia, an arbitration tribunal was set up to decide the location of the common frontier between Saudi Arabia and Abu Dhabi and the sovereignty of the Buraimi Oasis. Almost from the outset the United Kingdom has had reason to complain of the breaches of the conditions of arbitration which were agreed upon by the parties in an exchange of Notes. All diplomatic representations on these complaints to the Saudi Government having been without result, the United Kingdom was compelled to ask that the tribunal should consider these complaints at the meeting in Geneva in September.

The main charges which the United Kingdom made against Saudi Arabia were that the latter had tried to overthrow the ruler of Abu Dhabi by force, in favour of a Saudi nominee, and that they had been engaged in a deliberate, systematic, and persistent policy of large-scale bribery calculated to subvert the people in the disputed areas from their allegiance to the ruler of Abu Dhabi or the Sultan of Muscat.

Evidence of the Saudi attempt to promote a *coup d'état* in Abu Dhabi was given by Shaikh Hazza, the present ruler's brother. This evidence showed that some time last year the cadet branch of the ruling family, which is not well disposed towards the present ruler, went to Saudi Arabia, where they were given a very large sum of money and facilities for obtaining arms. On their return to Dubai, a shaikhdom bordering on Abu Dhabi, they attempted to secure support for an armed entry into Abu Dhabi with a view to overthrowing the present ruler. Counsel for Saudi Arabia did not even attempt to refute this evidence.

Although evidence showed that as much as 5,000 rupees a month was being paid by the Saudis to certain individuals as the price of their adherence to the Saudi cause, the campaign of bribery was particularly directed against members of the ruling family of Abu Dhabi, notably Shaikh Zayed bin Sultan, also a brother of the present ruler of Abu Dhabi and his representative in Buraimi. The Saudi agent was Abdullah al Quraishi, ostensibly a clerk in the Saudi police at Buraimi, but known to be a political officer high in the Saudi service.

Quraishi told Shaikh Zayed on March 30 that he had heard from the arbitration tribunal that the territory would be returned to the Saudis, and promised that if he would throw in his lot with the Saudis, he would be assured of his position in Buraimi, and would receive funds from the Saudis and 50 per cent of the profits from any oil that might be discovered there. Quraishi also said that should the arbitration go against the Saudis they would take the area by force.

Later an emissary from Quraishi offered him a new car and 40,000 rupees. The offer of 40,000 rupees was subsequently repeated by Quraishi himself, who said that it would be a present from King Saud. At a further meeting between Zayed and Quraishi on August 4, Quraishi said that King Saud would give Zayed 400 million rupees if he would prevent the Iraq Petroleum Company from operating in the disputed territories and leave the field open to ARAMCO (the oil company holding the concession for Saudi Arabia). King Saud would like to give a written guarantee to this effect, but was afraid to do so lest it should fall into British hands.

Shaikh Zayed loyally reported these approaches to his brother, the ruler of Abu Dhabi, and to Captain Clayton, the commander of the Abu Dhabi and Muscat police detachment in the Buraimi zone. Captain Clayton was called as witness before the tribunal and corroborated the Shaikh's evidence. Neither witness was shaken in cross-examination.

A similar attempt at bribery was made against two of the principal shaikhs of the Dhawahir tribe. They were approached by Shaikh Rashid bin Hamad, a Saudi partisan, who offered them a monthly payment of 100,000 rupees each if they would turn away from Abu Dhabi and declare for Saudi Arabia.

Counsel for Saudi Arabia did not attempt to deny that substantial sums of money had been distributed in the Buraimi Oasis. Instead, he described this as the bounty and generosity of the wealthy Arabs in this area. If there were Arabs in Buraimi able to distribute money on this scale they can only have got it from Saudi Arabia. This is a point with which counsel for Saudi Arabia did not deal.

Saudi Arabia made no attempt to refute the evidence of Shaikh Hazza or of the two shaikhs of the Dhawahir tribe. They did, however, call as a witness Abdullah al Quraishi. He admitted that there had been meetings between himself and Shaikh Zayed but said that they were asked for by Shaikh Zayed because he wanted advice about how to make his peace with Saudi Arabia. Quraishi denied that there had ever been any offers of money to Shaikh Zayed. He claimed that, although he was meeting Shaikh Zayed, against whom the Saudi Government had been making all kinds of complaints and who is their chief opponent in the oasis, he had never thought it necessary to report the meetings to the commander of the Saudi police detachment in Buraimi or to the Saudi Government.

Possessing as they did the strongest evidence (which has still not been refuted) that Saudi Arabia was engaged in a campaign of systematic corruption designed to pervert the arbitration, her Majesty's Government laid their case before the tribunal at Geneva. Unfortunately it soon became apparent that Saudi methods, which are now well known in the Middle East, were to be extended to the tribunal itself. Not only had Shaikh Yusuf Yasin to be called to order by the president for sending a note to the Saudi Agent (Quraishi) during the sitting of the tribunal, but Quraishi admitted under cross-examination that his first act on arriving in Geneva was to get in touch with Shaikh Yusuf Yasin, the Saudi member of the tribunal. There can be little doubt that the evidence he subsequently gave was carefully rehearsed with the Saudi arbitrator.

As it appears from the statement which Sir Reader Bullard made on his resignation from the tribunal, Shaikh Yusuf Yasin made it abundantly clear that it was he who was conducting the proceedings on behalf of the Saudi Arabian Government and was representing that Government on the tribunal rather than acting as an impartial arbitrator. He was in fact the judge of his own cause.

Moreover, he asserted that Quraishi was his official, for whose acts in Buraimi he accepted responsibility. In spite of this he claimed that during the period of the Quraishi-Zayed interviews mentioned above he had 'forgotten' to take action on three British protests against the presence of Quraishi in the Buraimi zone. Finally, confirmation was secured of Her Majesty's Government's suspicion that attempts had been made by the Saudis to tamper with the impartiality of the tribunal behind the president's back.*

In these circumstances, Sir Reader Bullard had no choice but to declare that he could not continue as a member of the arbitration tribunal. Her Majesty's Government are in full agreement with the motives that led to Sir Reader Bullard's action.

The president of the tribunal, Dr Charles de Visscher, has also felt it necessary to resign and her Majesty's Government wish to record their appreciation of his services and their regret that this distinguished jurist should have been placed in so difficult a position.

The Times 5 October 1955

*Senor Ernesto de Dihaigo, the Cuban member of the tribunal later revealed that he had been approached in an attempt to influence him and his resignation followed that of the chairman. Despite his earlier denials of any approaches to him during his pilgrimage, Mr Mohammad Hassan of Pakistan, the other independent member of the tribunal was the last to resign.

15

The Prime Minister's Statement to the House of Commons on the Failure of Arbitration in the Buraimi Dispute on 26 October 1955

Sir Anthony Eden said: The House may recall that on July 28, 1954 I reported that agreement had been reached with the Saudi Arabian Government to submit the Buraimi frontier dispute to arbitration. I expressed the hope that this agreement would enable us to resume the traditionally friendly relations between her Majesty's Government and the Saudi Arabian Government. I am sorry to have to tell the House that these hopes have been disappointed. The proceedings before the arbitration tribunal at Geneva have broken down, and the British member of the tribunal and its Belgian president have resigned. The reasons for these events were explained in detail in a statement issued by the Foreign Office on October 4. I have just heard that Dr Dihigo, one of the two remaining members of the tribunal appointed as a neutral, has also resigned.

For many years her Majesty's Government sought to reach an agreement in these matters by negotiation with the Saudi Arabian Government. These efforts led only to steadily increased Saudi claims against the territory of two Arab rulers, the Ruler of Abu Dhabi and the Sultan of Muscat. Finally, in August 1952, in the region of Buraimi, the Saudi official Turki bin Ataishan, after passing through the territory of the Ruler of Abu Dhabi, invaded the territory of the Sultan of Muscat and established himself in a village belonging to the Sultan.

In spite of this provocative act, her Majesty's Government continued to seek a solution by peaceful means, and dissuaded those local leaders who wished to meet force by force. For two years Turki remained in Buraimi, seeking to extend Saudi influence in the area.

In 1954 her Majesty's Government advised the two Arab rulers to submit their case to arbitration. An arbitration agreement was drawn up which, it was hoped, would lead to a settlement and to more friendly relations.

The Saudi Arabian authorities have systematically disregarded the conditions of arbitration which were then agreed upon. The 'police' group which they were permitted to keep in the Buraimi Oasis for the sole purpose of maintaining law and order was in fact led by political officers who persistently exceeded their functions. Bribery and intimidation on a wide scale has taken place in the disputed areas, with the result that it is no longer possible, I regret to say, to estimate where the loyalties of the inhabitants lay before Turki's armed incursion.

The Ruler of Abu Dhabi and the Sultan of Muscat have scrupulously observed the conditions of arbitration which her Majesty's Government in good faith recommended to them. They have had to stand by and watch their subjects being suborned, and the outcome of the arbitration itself being gravely prejudiced in advance. A fair and impartial arbitration is not possible in such circumstances.

These facts, combined with the conduct of the Saudi Government in relation to the tribunal itself, have led her Majesty's Government to conclude that the Saudi Arabian Government are no more willing now to reach an equitable solution by arbitration than they were previously by negotiation. Their actions and conduct amount to a repudiation of the arbitration agreement, and have made a continuation of the arbitration impossible.

Her Majesty's Government have therefore felt obliged in the exercise of its duty, which is to protect the legitimate interests of the Ruler of Abu Dhabi and the Sultan of Muscat to advise them that the attempt to reach a just compromise by means of arbitration has failed. The forces of these rulers, supported by the Trucial Oman Levies, have accordingly this morning taken steps to resume their previous control of the Buraimi oasis, and areas to the west of it. My latest information is that the Saudi force has been evacuated from the Buraimi oasis, their only casualties being two men slightly wounded. They are being cared for by our forces.

Her Majesty's Government and the rulers concerned have no doubt that, as a matter of law, they would be entitled to regard as a fair frontier between the Ruler of Abu Dhabi and Saudi Arabia the line many in this House know as the 1952 line, claimed in their recent memorial before the tribunal. However, while fully reserving their legal rights in that respect, they have decided, with the agreement of the rulers, in order to act in as reasonable and conciliatory a manner as possible, to declare and uphold a line which is more favourable to Saudi Arabia.

In 1935, when the present dispute may be said to have crystallized, a line, which is known as the Riyadh line, was put forward by her Majesty's Government. It involved substantial concessions to the Saudi Arabians. This line was further modified in 1937 in favour of Saudi Arabia, and it is this modified line that we are now declaring as the frontier. The Saudi Arabian Government is being informed of these decisions.

I regret that this step should have been necessary. But, as negotiations and arbitration have both failed, we have no other means of honouring our obligations and standing by our friends. I hope that in time the Saudi Arabian Government will accept the solution that we have had to declare. Her Majesty's Government are ready at all times to discuss with the Saudi Arabian Government any minor rectifications of the line which may seem convenient in the light of local circumstances.

The Times 26 October 1955

16

The Saudi Arabian Government's statement on the Buraimi Oasis Dispute 13 November 1955

The three tribal chiefs, who arrived in Dammam (Saudi Arabia) recently, explained that a British military force, led by British Officers, besieged suddenly the two villages of Buraimi and Hamasa before the dawn prayers and asked their inhabitants to surrender.

The people of the territory refused to obey such orders and declared that they were since long, the followers of the house of Saud and still owned allegiance to His Majesty King Saud.

The tribal chiefs explained that they were deputed by the Saudi Royal family as such and that it was quite impossible for them to deviate from the allegiance to the Saudi monarch since the territory was rightly considered to be an integral part of Saudi Arabia.

Consequently, fighting took place between the British forces and the inhabitants, and it continued for about 14 hours until the inhabitants had consumed their last bullet and, therefore had to surrender.

The chiefs confirmed that the British forces suffered loss of not less than 82 soldiers and a number of Arabs who were compelled by the British authorities to fight their brethren. Some of the Arabs who tried to avoid the clash with their fellowmen of the territory were shot down by the British soldiers at the rear.

Later on the British forces led Sheikh Saqar Bin Sultan, Sheikh Bin Hamad and the son of Sheikh Abid bin Jammah to the British Headquarters and compelled them to present Sheikh Abid Bin Jammah himself. They also asked them to surrender all the arms owned by the inhabitants.

After the arms were surrendered, the British forces entered the two village and started looting, including what belonged to the ladies.

The British then demanded from the tribal chiefs to pay allegiance to Britain and to the Sheikh of Muescat, promising them the return of their properties as well as their liberation.

The chiefs refused the offer and reiterated their allegiance to their religious leader and King, His Majesty King Saud. The British tried in vain to persuade them individually to accept their terms.

The tribal chiefs were then told that if they chose to travel to Saudi Arabia, all their properties would be confiscated and they would never be allowed to return home. The tribal chiefs gladly chose to travel to Saudi Arabia which they consider as their ancestral land.

Sheikh Abid and Sheikh Rashid left for Saudi Arabia while Sheik Saqar was detained by the British forces in an effort to win him over and secure his allegiance to them. Again they failed.

Before their departure the three tribal chiefs had to hear Billingsgate language.

In spite of these facts, the British Foreign Minister has stated in the House of Commons that the occupation of the Buraimi Oasis was executed without any incident and that the state of affairs in the territory was satisfactory.

APP 13 November 1955

17

Planned Re-organisation of the TOS for 1959

The new establishment was to be:

Personnel

1 TOS (less Medical Centre and Workshops)

42 x British Officers
77 x British Other Ranks
33 x Arab Officers
1075 x Arab Other Ranks
92 x Enlisted Followers
50 x Boys
14 x Civilians

2 TOS Medical Centre

3 x British Officers (RAMC)
14 x British Other Ranks (RAMC)
36 x Arab Other Ranks
11 x Enlisted Followers

3 TOS Workshops

3 x British Officers (REME)
30 x British Other Ranks (REME)
71 x Arab Other Ranks
8 x Enlisted Followers

4 TOTAL

47 x British Officers
121 x British Other Ranks
33 x Arab Officers
1182 x Arab Other Ranks
111 x Enlisted Followers
50 x Boys
14 x Civilians

Vehicles

	Phase I	Phase II	Medical	Workshops	Total
Car Heavy Utility 4 x 4	1				1
Truck ¼-ton 4 x 4 FFW	10	6		1	17
Truck ¼-ton 4 x 4 GS	61	31	11	2	105
Truck 1-ton 4 x 4 Water	8	3	1		12
Truck 1-ton 4 x 4 Welding				1	1
Truck 3-ton 4 x 4 GS Cargo	68	16	1	2	87
Truck 3-ton 4 x 4 Repair				1	1
Truck 3-ton 4 x 4 Tele- com repair				1	1
Tractor 6 x 6 Heavy Recovery				2	2
Crane Mobile 3 ton				1	1

Organisation

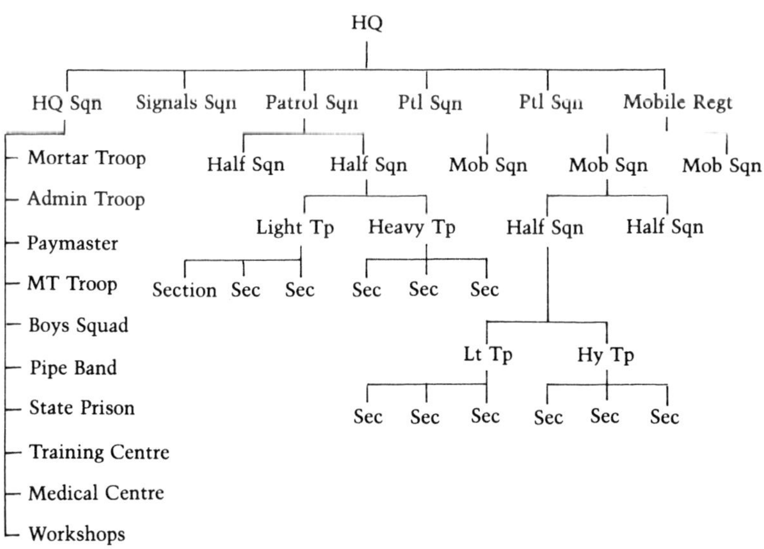

TOS Headquarters

Commander	Colonel	(British)
Deputy Commander	Lieutenant-Colonel	(British)
	responsible for HQ, Training and independent patrol squadrons	
Brigade Major	Major	(British)
DAA & QMG	Major	(British)
Intelligence Officer	Major and Captain	(British)
Defence troop	Sergeant and 2 x sections	

Patrol Squadron

Squadron HQ	Major (British) CQMS (British) SSM WO2 SQMS S/Sergeant Cooks x 3 Storeman Orderly Clerk Drivers, Corporal and 9 Sweepers dry x 2 Sweeper wet Tailor Water carrier
Half Squadron HQ	Captain (British) Orderly
Light Troop HQ	Mulazim Troop Sergeant Orderly
Sections x 3	Corporal and 4 x Private Soldiers
Heavy Troop HQ	Mulazim Troop Sergeant Orderly
Sections x 3	Corporal, Lance Corporal, 5 x Privates

Transport	Truck 1/4-ton 4 x 4 FFW (Commander) Truck 1/4-ton 4 x 4 GS x 5 (Patrol duties) Truck 1-ton 4 x 4 Water Trucks 3-ton 4 x 4 GS x 3 (Troop carriers)
Total Personnel	3 x British Officers 1 x British NCO 4 x Arab Officers 6 x Arab NCOs 94 x Arab Rank and File 5 x Enlisted Followers

Mobile Regiment Headquarters

Commander	Lieutenant-Colonel (British)
Adjutant	Captain (British)
Signals Officer	Captain (British)
Intelligence Officer	Mulazim
Clerk	Corporal (British)
Regimental Sergeant Major	WO1
Orderlies x 4	
Clerks GD x 2	
CQMS	S/Sergeant (British)
Storemen x 2	
Cooks x 2	
Drivers	Corporals x 4 Lance Corporals x 4 Privates x 28
Transport	Trucks 1/4-ton FFW x 4 (Commander, Adjutant, Signals Officer, IO) Trucks 1/4-ton 4 x 4 GS x 21 (increment to move 3 squadrons) Truck 1-ton 4 x 4 Water Trucks 3-ton 4 x 4 GS Cargo x 6 (Ammunition, Fuels, Rations, Stores plus increment to move three squadrons)

Mobile Squadron

Squadron HQ	Major (British) SSM WO2 SQMS S/Sergeant Drivers x 7 Cooks x 3 Orderly Clerk GD Sweeper wet Sweepers dry x 2 Tailor Water Carrier
Transport	Truck ¼-ton 4 x 4 GS (Commander) Truck ¼-ton 4 x 4 FFW (C12 wireless) Truck ¼-ton 4 x 4 FFW (201 wireless) Truck 1-ton 4 x 4 Water Truck 3-ton 4 x 4 GS Cargo
Mobile Half Squadron HQ	Captain (British) Orderly Driver
Transport	Truck ¼-ton 4 x 4 GS
Light Troop HQ	Mulazim Troop sergeant Orderly Driver
Transport	Truck ¼-ton 4 x 4 GS
Sections x 3	Corporal Lance Corporal Privates x 4 Driver
Transport	Truck ¼-ton 4 x 4 GS

Heavy Troop HQ	Mulazim Troop Sergeant Orderly Driver
Sections x 3	Corporal Lance Corporal Privates x 5
Transport	Truck 3-ton 4 x 4 GS Cargo (or Dodge Power-Wagons x 3)
Total Personnel	3 x British Officers 4 x Arab Officers 6 x Arab NCOs 103 x Arab Rank and File 5 x Enlisted Followers

Training Centre

HQ	Major (British) Instructor Sergeant APTC (British) Clerk GD
	Cooks x 2 Kitchen boys x 2 Sweeper wet Sweepers dry x 3 Tailor Waiters x 2 Water carrier
Recruit Training	Wing (60 to 80 recruits) Captain (British) Instructor Sergeants x 2 (British) Training Officer Mulazim Instructor S/Sergeant Instructor Sergeants x 3 Instructor Corporals x 6

Weapon Training Wing (20 to 30 students)
Captain (British)
Instructor Sergeants x 2 (British)
Training Officer Mulazim
Instructor S/Sergeant
Instructor Sergeant
Instructor Corporals x 3
Orderlies x 2

Tactical Training Wing (20 to 30 students)
Captain (British)
Instructor Sergeant (British)
Training Officer Mulazim
Instructor S/Sergeant
Instructor Sergeants x 3
Orderlies x 2

Medical Centre (30 Beds Arab)
Officer Commanding Major RAMC
Regimental Medical Officer RAMC
Wardmaster WO2 RAMC

Administration	Sergeant Clerk RAMC Segeant Steward RAMC Sergeant Nurse RAMC
Training	S/Sergeant RAMC
Dental Centre	Dental Officer RADC Dental Technician Corporal RADC Dental Clerk/Assistant Corporal RADC
Medical Unit	Medical Officer RAMC Medical Sergeant RAMC Medical Corporal RAMC Medical Orderly Corporal Medical Orderly Lance Corporal Medical Orderlies x 6 Drivers x 2

Each Squadron (x 6)
Medical Orderly Corporal

Transport	Trucks ¼-ton 4 x 4 Stretcher x 10
	Trucks ¼-ton 4 x 4 GS x 3
	Truck 1-ton 4 x 4 Water
	Truck 3-ton 4 x 4 GS Cargo
	Trailer ½-ton Cargo
	Trailer ½-ton Water

18

Glossary

Military Ranks

Sahib — The form of address for British officers. British officers and other ranks were addressed by their English titles eg 'Major sahib', 'Sergeant Smith'. Arab ranks were addressed after the old Turkish style brought by the Arab Legion from Jordan:

Mulazim Awal – Lieutenant
Mulazim Thani – 2nd Lieutenant
Wakil – Warrant Officer or Sergeant Major
Shawish – Sergeant
Areef – Corporal
Jundi Awal – Lance Corporal
Jundi – Private Soldier

Weapons

Haun — A Mortar, eg 'Haun toohinch' is a two-inch Mortar.

Kanad — British Army Rifle .303-inch No 4 bolt action 10-round magazine introduced into service 1940. Used by the TOL and TOS and a few had been supplied to some shaikhs' guards.

Sharaf — British Army Rifle .303-inch SMLE Mk III bolt action 10-round magazine introduced into service 1907. The most widely available modern rifle used by Shaikhs' retainers and other civilians. In most cases, the forestock had been cut away: either straight across just forward of the outer band to leave the barrel exposed and the foresight protectors removed, as favoured in the Trucial States; or tapered from just forward of the magazine to the muzzle, with the foresight protectors and bayonet boss removed and with a replacement outer band fitted, favoured in Saudi Arabia for those weapons supplied by the UK during and after the Arab Revolt in 1916.

Barashute — British Army Rifle .303-inch No 5 Jungle carbine was developed from the No 4 for use in the Far East late in the Second World War, it has a conical flash hider. Some of these were found in use by the Omani rebels in 1957, presumably supplied by Saudi Arabia but unlikely to have been part of a direct consignment to Saudi Arabia from the UK as had been the No 3 SMLEs.

Sama' — Single-shot Martini action .45-inch carbine mostly of 19th-century origin that was carried by the majority of civilians outside the towns. The ammunition generally available was many-times-used brass cartridge cases refilled with locally made black gunpowder with a locally made lead bullet, the primer cap being filled with the composition taken from the red Swan Vesta matchhead for preference. When lead was in short supply, the bullet was made of a metal strip, tightly rolled with only the nose dipped into milten lead. When fired at close range from a weapon with any rifling remaining in the barrel, the projectile could unwind with devastating effect on any target hit.

Sakitoon — Any .22-inch calibre weapon.

Vehicles

Bidfa — Bedford QL truck 4 x 4 3-ton GS Cargo

Doj — Dodge 4 x 4 Power-Wagon

Kenwar — Kenworth truck as used by ARAMCO

Landroval — (plural *Landroveraat*) Landrover 4 x 4 $\frac{1}{4}$-ton

Maaris	(plural *Mowaris*) Morris 4 x 4 truck 1-ton
Shefer	Chevrolet-made vehicle
Taxi	Any saloon car
Mechanical Terms	
Banna	Spanner. Sometimes 'sevensixteen *kabir* (or *soghrir*') for the double-ended, open-jaw tool.
Delco	The distributor of a petrol engine, from the name embossed on the top of the distributor cap of the vehicles of American origin, such as the Ford and Chevrolet, first used in the Arab world.
Dynamo start	The starter motor, in contrast to:
Dynamo kahraba	or *Dynamo sharj* – the generator
Manuela	The starting handle of a motor car. Origin probably from the 'manual start' of the old Ford Model T cars that were first worked on by Arab mechanics in Egypt and the word was handed down.
Miftah ingleezi	Adjustable spanner
Seer punka	Fan belt
Skrubanna	or *Skrudrival* – Screwdriver
Stebni	Spare wheel (Stepney)

Other

'Abra	A ferry
'Agal	A headrope
'Aqabat	A mountain pass or defile
Amir	Ruler's representative in the Trucial States, used west of the mountains. In Oman and on the eastern coast known as Wali
'Azima	A formal feast of honour, literally, 'an invitation'
Bait	A house or other dwelling
Barusti	A house built of palm fronds, palm-frond panels used for building
Bedu	Used to describe a nomadic individual, or group. Adjectival form is *bedui*. Anglicised to bedouin in singular and plural
Chandal	A mangrove pole
Chagul	A canvas water bag

Charpoy	Indian name for wood-framed string bed
Dhabi	A type of gazelle
Dhow	Generic term used in English for larger Arab craft and boats
Dhubb	A desert lizard (square-headed monitor)
Falaj	An underground water conduit
Gerzaiya soof	A military 'Jersey wool pullover'
Ghaf	Species of tree
Haaf	'Shorts PT', sometimes 'Drawers Cellular'
Hagana	Camel troops
Hazza	A pass through a range of sand dunes
Jabal	A mountain or hill
Jumbeeng	Corrugated or other rough desert surface
Kaboot	A military 'Greatcoat, ORs'
Khaima	A tent or temporary shelter
Khanjar	A dagger
Koop	A 'Mug, enamel ½ pint'
Mangaria	A soldier's Mess tin
Mazri	Blue-grey lightweight wool cloth, of Indian origin, adopted by TOS for their shirts
Melkh inglizi	Epsom Salts
Meza	A low, flat-topped outcrop of harder rock on otherwise flat ground, resulting from erosion
Naib	Early word for sergeant, meaning deputy
Qitt	Bed-bugs
Rafiq	A travelling companion responsible for the safety of his charges in tribal territory
Ramlet	A defined sand feature
Ras	A head or headland
Sabkhat	Salt marsh, usually without vegetation. The top crust after having been broken would re-form with time and when wet
Samara	A species of thorn tree
Sangar	Defensive stone breastwork, often around a hollow
Shaikh	A tribal leader, also used as a title for a religious teacher
Shmagh	A headcloth, usually red (or other colour) and white check, as worn by the military
Sih	A plain, usually gravel

Suq	A market
Tamima	A paramount shaikh
Tawi	A well
Thaub	A cloaklike garment
Wadi	A valley
Wali	A ruler's representative or local governor
Wasima	A medal or decoration
Wasm	A brand mark on camels, 'logo' on vehicles etc
Wazra	A loincloth
Zariba	A protective thorn hedge used in Sudan and East Africa against wild animals
Zamzamiya	A water bottle

19

Abbreviations

ADMA	Abu Dhabi Marine Areas (Oil Company)
AOR	Arab Other Rank
AIOC	Anglo-Iranian Oil Company
ALO	(RAF) Air Liaison Officer (with ground troops)
APA	Arab Political Assistant
APL	Aden Protectorate Levies
APTC	Army Physical Training Corps
ARAMCO	Arabian American (Oil) Company
BBME	British Bank of the Middle East
BER	Beyond Economical Repair (of military equipment)
BM	Brigade Major (General Staff Officer, Grade 2)
BOAC	British Overseas Airways Corporation
BOR	British Other Rank
CO	Commanding Officer (of a military unit)
COMTOS	Commandant Trucial Oman Scouts
CRS	Casualty Reception Station
CW	Carrier Wave
DAA +	Deputy Assistant Adjutant and Quartermaster General
QMG	(Administrative Staff Officer, Grade 2)
DIO	Desert Intelligence Officer
DLS	Desert Locust Survey
DP	Drill Purpose
FO	Foreign Office, Whitehall, London
GD	General Duty
GHQ	General Head Quarters
GLO	(Army) Ground Liaison Officer (for air operations)
GS	General Service
GSO 1	General Staff Officer Grade 1
HMG	Her Majesty's Government
HMS	Her Majesty's Ship

HQLFPG	Head Quarters Land Forces Persian Gulf
HQLLFPG	Head Quarters Local Land Forces Persian Gulf
IAL	International Aeradio Limited
IO	Intelligence Officer
IOTOS	Intelligence Officer of the Trucial Oman Scouts
IPC	Iraq Petroleum Company
JIB	Joint Intelligence Bureau
KD	Khadi Drill (textile)
KRRC	King's Royal Rifle Corps
LDC	Local Defence Committee
LIC	Local Intelligence Committee
LST	Landing Ship (Tank)
Lieut	Lieutenant
Lieut-Col	Lieutenant Colonel
MAF	Muscat Armed Forces
MCW	Modulated Carrier Wave
MEAF	Middle East Air Forces
MECAS	Middle East Centre for Arabic Studies
MELF	Middle East Land Forces
MFF	Muscat Field Force
MO4	War Office branch for Middle East Operations
MOFF	Muscat and Oman Field Force
MT	Motor Transport
MTO	Motor Transport Officer
NCO	Non-Commissioned Officer
NFR	Northern Frontier Regiment (of SAF)
OC	Officer Commanding (of a military sub-unit)
ORQMS	Orderly Room Quarter Master Sergeant (Chief Clerk)
PA	Political Agent
PDO	Petroleum Development (Oman)
PDTC	Petroleum Development (Trucial Coast)
PFLOAG	Popular Front for the Liberation of Oman and the Persian Gulf
PO	Political Officer
PR	British Political Resident, Persian Gulf
PRO	Public Records Office
PT	Physical Training
ptl	Patrol
QL	Bedford QL truck 4 x 4
QM	Quarter Master (Stores Officer)

RADC	Royal Army Dental Corps
RAF	Royal Air Force
RAMC	Royal Army Medical Corps
RE	Royal Engineers
regt	Regiment
REME	Royal Electrical and Mechanical Engineers
RL	Bedford RL truck 4 x 4 – replaced the QL
RN	Royal Navy
RSM	Regimental Sergeant Major (WO I)
RQMS	Regimental Quarter Master Sergeant
SAF	Sultan (of Oman's) Armed Forces
SAOPG	Senior Army Officer Persian Gulf
SAS	Special Air Service Regiment
sec	Section
SDIO	Senior Desert Intelligence Officer
Sgt	Sergeant
SNOPG	Senior Naval Officer Persian Gulf
SOAF	Sultan of Oman's Air Force
sqn	Squadron
SRAFOPG	Senior Royal Air Force Officer Persian Gulf
SS	Steam ship
S/Sgt	Staff Sergeant or Colour Sergeant
SSM	Squadron Sergeant Major
SQMS	Squadron Quartermaster Sergeant
Tac HQ	Tactical Head Quarters
TOL	Trucial Oman Levies
TOS	Trucial Oman Scouts
tp	Troop
UAE	United Arab Emirates
UAR	United Arab Republic
UN	United Nations
WO	Warrant Officer Class I or II
WS	Wireless Station
2i/c	Second-in-Command

Bibliography

Unpublished

1 Foreign Office records FO371, years 1949 to 1961 inclusive. In Public Records Office, Kew.

2 Arabic text: 'The exchange of letters and the agreement to arbitration to resolve the dispute concerning the area of Buraimi and concerning the frontiers in disagreement between the Kingdom of Saudi Arabia and Abu Dhabi'. Saudi Arabian Ministry of the Exterior 1954. In my possession.

Published

Long Range Desert Group, W B Kennedy Shaw, Collins 1945.

The Golden Rubble, Roderic Owen, Collins 1957.

Soldier Magazine, HM Stationery Office, January 1956.

Sultan in Oman, James Morris, Faber & Faber 1957.

Arabian Sands, Wilfred Thesiger, Longman 1959.

Arabian Adventure, Anthony Shepherd, Collins 1961.

Warlords of Arabia, Phillip Allfree, Robert Hale 1967.

Arabian Assignment, David Smiley, Leo Cooper Ltd 1975.

Courtesies in the Gulf Area, Donald Horley, Stacey International 1978.

From Trucial States to United Arab Emirates, Frauke Heard-Bey, Longman Group 1982.

One Man's SAS, Lofty Large, William Kimber 1987.

This Strange Eventful History, Edward Henderson, Quartet Books Ltd 1988.

The Seven Shaikhdoms, Ronald Codrai, Stacey International 1990.